IGNORANCE
AND
KNOWLEDGE
FOE AND FRIEND

TRUTH AND LIFE MOTIVATION

E. T. EZEKIEL

Order this book online at www.trafford.com
or email orders@trafford.com

Most Trafford titles are also available at major online book retailers.

Printed in the United States of America.

ISBN: 978-1-4907-1227-7 (sc)
ISBN: 978-1-4907-1226-0 (e)

Trafford rev. 10/04/2013

 www.trafford.com

North America & international
toll-free: 1 888 232 4444 (USA & Canada)
fax: 812 355 4082

Contents

DEDICATION

This book is dedicated to Almighty God—who made the heavens and the earth and created man in His own image to have dominion over all other things created. He is the beginning and the end, who showed His love by giving us His only begotten Son to die for our sin so that we might be saved and gave the right to as many that believed Him and believe in His name to become children of God, who sealed us for the day of redemption by His Holy Spirit.

PREFACE

I have seen mysterious things happening—tragedies and joy, failure and success, prosperity and destruction all happening to men.

For years now, I have being studying the life of people and have realized that all the things happening in this world are as a result of ignorance and knowledge. The good thing that gives life to men is initiated by knowledge, while the bad ones that destroy are caused by ignorance which is lack of knowledge.

In this book, the Bible passage that really pointed out the main problem faced by humanity was quoted; Hosea 4:6 says, "My people are destroyed for lack of knowledge . . . ." Here, God is actually referring to His people or chosen ones. We may say, the so-called children of God. But the question is why will the people who are called God's children still get into judgment of destruction, since it is God who created all things, has all good things, and owns all powers?

The simple answer is exactly what God said. If we read further, we will discover that the priest was mentioned. This means no one was left behind in this matter.

The issue of ignorance and knowledge is a great issue that does not only attack the people who did not know or believe in God but also the people who knows and believes.

This book will give you the deep meaning and truths about ignorance and knowledge. This book will also open your eyes of understanding to weapons that ignorance uses to capture its victim and how to be free from them.

God bless you as you read.

All scriptures are quoted from the King James Version of the Bible.

CHAPTER ONE

IGNORANCE AND KNOWLEDGE

W e can't discuss this topic without making the Bible our reference. This is because knowledge is from God. So if I decide to tell you things about ignorance and knowledge without God, then you will be wasting your time reading lies, and what I will be saying may not profit you. But I want to tell you the truth so that it can give you life as the name of our motivational ministry. It is essential that I tell you the truth so that you can get life.

Ignorance is a great killer. Many lives have been wasted just because of ignorance. Some would have been greater than their present stage, but ignorance has made them to remain a failure.

Ignorance simply means lack of knowledge. That is, it is the opposite of knowledge. We can also say ignorance is lack of education, understanding, or experience. Ignorance can also be described as unawareness. That is, un-inform or unknown.

Ignorance is from the word "ignore." Ignore means neglects, pay no attention, reject, unnoticed, pass over, overlook, etcetera. We can say ignorance is when knowledge is ignored. And the truth is when knowledge is ignored, ignorance is always noted.

Many are living below their expectation because of ignorance. Ignorance is a silent killer. It can be likened to a termite that descends on a very large pluck of wood, and some days later, it finishes it up.

1

The greatest enemy that must be faced in human race is ignorance. God talks about ignorance in Hosea 4:6. "My people are destroyed for lack of knowledge: because thou hast rejected knowledge, I will also reject thee, that thou shall be no priest to me: seeing thou hast forgotten the law of thy God, I will also forget thy children."

From this passage, we can see that the people of God did not perish because of lack of power, strength, anointing, money, riches, wealth, opportunity, position, etcetera. But they perish because of lack of knowledge which is ignorance.

Knowledge can be likened to an enclosed container or vessel containing all things pertaining to life. It is a platform that our life depends on. It is a platform that all the good things of life depend on. It is just like a part of a helicopter that is called Jesus nut, which is located at the top of the fan blade. According to the engineers, when the nut becomes loose, the next thing you will see is Jesus, and you will only see Jesus if you are righteous or holy because the Bible says without holiness, no one will see the LORD (Heb. 12:14).

Without knowledge, one is as good as dead. Everything you need to know in order to survive or to live is inside knowledge. Until you seek for it and open it, you will be ignorant of that particular thing needed.

Knowledge and ignorance are contrary words that can never agree. They are enemies. You can never be on both sides at the same time. You are either knowledgeable or ignorant. Wherever knowledge appears, ignorance disappears, and where knowledge is lacking, ignorance will dominate.

It is possible to be ignorant and still not know or be aware. This actually means you may be blinded by your ignorance. This situation happens when you know nothing and still believe to have known all. You must understand that we learn different things every day. Then, it will be very wrong for you to believe you have known all when you are supposed to keep on learning. This is a high level of ignorance.

Many would have been free from the bondage they are now, if only they are able to get much or little knowledge. Ignorance is a disease which must be cured. And as you know, diseases are not friendly. They must be killed instantly as soon as they are discovered so that there would be no chance for them to dominate, talk less of killing.

Some nations are still in bondage because of ignorance that has not been eradicated. And because ignorance is ruling some nations, many destinies have been wasted.

Ignorance is a spirit used by the devil to destroy destiny. That's just the truth. It does not matter whether you believe it or not. It is a tool used by the devil to destroy mankind. When it dominates a person's life, then it becomes the person's character.

All things have been created since the foundation of the world. No new thing is being or to be created. That is, God has created everything you are seeing every day and in every generation and even the one to come. That is why scientists don't create, but discover. The word discover simply means to find something that was hidden. But a blind person can't even see what is around him or her, talk less of finding or discovering what has been hidden, because his or her eyes have been covered with veil.

Anything you are ignorant of will have power over you and can do anything it wishes to you. It is knowledge that brings freedom. Ignorance is a modern and common bondage that has imprisoned many. It is impossible to protest against ignorance because it is a force that cannot be defeated with human power. The only force that can destroy ignorance is knowledge. The wickedness of ignorance is that it does not imprison people for nothing but for destruction.

1 Corinthians 2:12 say, "Now we have received, not the spirit of the world, but the Spirit which is of God; that we might know the things that are freely given to us of God." This means God has given things to us freely without any charge just like what the Bible say in Genesis 1:28-30 *(and God blessed them, and God said unto them, Be fruitful, and multiply, and replenish the earth, and subdue it; and have dominion over the fish of the sea, and over the fowl of the air, and over every living thing that moveth upon the earth. And God said, behold, I have given you every herb bearing seed, which is upon the face of all the earth, and every tree, in which is the fruit of a tree yielding seed; to you it shall be for meat. And to every beast of the earth, and to every fowl of the air; and to everything that creepeth upon the earth, wherein there is life, I have given every green herb for meat: and it was so).* So God gave us all things to control, not only the things which we can see, but also things that are invisible to our physical eyes including the gifts and talents in us.

But the devil stole the authority God gave us and hijacked those things that have been freely given to us. Remember I said talents and gifts of life are part of it. But thank God that Jesus came to restore us back; this is the reason why you see much development these days. However, it is only few that is fulfilling purpose. The devil uses the veil of ignorance to cover our faces so that we won't know what belongs to us and that instead of people to be prospering according to the commandment of God, they are perishing. But for me, I will say, I will not perish but prosper in Jesus's name. Ignorance is a veil the devil is using to cover people's eyes so that he can destroy them and wipe them off from the surface of the earth. When you are ignorant, you are already under the umbrella of the devil leading you to the place of destruction.

The truth of the matter is that knowledge is from God. It doesn't matter whether you believe this or not. Most of the knowledge in this world is ignorance because in the end, it destructs people. Knowledge does not destroy. It is a life. Any knowledge that destroys people or you perceive its end to be destruction is not knowledge or the real knowledge, but it is perverseness or ignorance disguised as knowledge. The only thing knowledge destroys is ignorance. I want you to know that ignorance can disguise itself as knowledge so that it gains the heart of many. No one wants to die, especially when it appears to us as death, but when it disguises, it captures and kills many. Devil won't tell you he is a devil but rather lie to you. Likewise ignorance won't appear to you as ignorance, because it is devil's agent. They are both liars. The Bible tells us that the devil is a liar and the father of it (John 8:44).

1 Corinthians 2:14 says "But the natural man receiveth not the things of the Spirit of God: for they are foolishness unto him: neither can he know them, because they are spiritually discerned." I said something earlier on that knowledge (the true or real knowledge) is from God. But the words of God say here that even a natural man or a carnal man cannot receive the true knowledge that is from God. According to the dictionary, natural means nature, usual, physical world, human nature, innate, not affected like real life, biological, and not sharp or flat. Knowledge is not something you get on a platter of gold; it is what you get by seeking and with humility. You have to go the extra

mile by doing what natural men don't do before getting the knowledge. It is also possible to go the extra mile and do an unusual things just to acquire abundance of ignorance. This issue is a serious matter that needs to be taught also in a spiritual manner.

CHAPTER TWO

LEVELS OF IGNORANCE

Now, the truth of the matter is that no one can claim to be completely free from ignorance. Why? Because we learn every day and we are supposed to be learning every day.

It is only the dead that are not learning anymore. We can say they are the one that are free from ignorance on earth.

It is either you are partially ignorant or completely ignorant.

1. Partially ignorant: This level of ignorance is when you lack knowledge of a particular thing or something because you did not seek or know. Nevertheless, you wish to be free and by so doing, you seek knowledge. This is like someone who is sick but trying all he could do to get free from the sickness. He may eventually get a solution. Why? Because he seeks solution and finds it. That is, he knew the truth that he was sick but did not accept the fact that he will be sick forever. He assumes the sickness to be temporary. This level of ignorance can be explained in a simpler way; when we are always ready to listen and learn new things although you may know little but always ready to get more knowledge. We can also explain this further to a person who has not been completely captured by ignorance.

2. Completely ignorant: This is high level of ignorance. People that fall into this category have been completely captured by ignorance. It is a level of ignorance whereby the person knew nothing or did not have access to the knowledge or is not ready to learn. The kind of people in this level always believes to be right at all time and are not ready to learn; in other words, they reject correction and knowledge. This category of people always argues wrongly, fights, quarrels despite being wrong, and always tries to confuse and initiate others. They always have wrong information, and when corrected, they cause conflict. These kinds of people are proud in nature. They always try to enslave people with their ignorance. They always do wrong things. They are traitors, wicked, and evildoers.

CHAPTER THREE

TRUTHS ABOUT IGNORANCE

In this chapter, we shall be discussing 120 truths one needs to know about ignorance.

1. It kills: Ignorance is a disease that kills gradually. When you fail to seek knowledge, you will become a victim of ignorance. It looks to be friendly, but its only mission is to blindfold and kill. Many won't have died if not for the ignorance of one thing or the other. The joy of it is that beside every lies, there is always the truth. Which means knowledge is always around us; it is just only for us to allow it so as to destroy the agendas and works or implications of ignorance.

2. It destroys or kills terribly: Many died a terrible death because of lack of knowledge. Ignorance does not kill gently or softly. Every death caused by ignorance is always terrible. Although doing somethings ignorantly maybe pleasant at the beginning, but the end is always worse. The best thing is to always run from ignorance when your eyes are open. As I have said, knowledge is always around and ready to assist us. And if it is not around, seek for it and you will find it. Although knowledge is willing to set some people free, but they have ignorantly sent it away. And the end of such is always terrible. Many have perished for lack of knowledge (Hosea 4:6).

3.   It is devil's messenger: Ignorance is one of the devices the devil uses to capture people and have succeeded in using it. He knows that once he succeeds in preventing people from seeking knowledge, it will be easy for him to do to them what he wishes. He makes sure he does not allow people to have access to knowledge and even does a great job by letting people to hate knowledge. Whenever you are ignorant of a particular thing, it means you are in darkness. And you know that it is easy to capture person in the darkness than the person in the light because the one in the dark won't even know where to go.

4.   It is an enemy of life: Wherever ignorance dominates, death is always present. The passage of the Bible we read earlier on says "My people perish for lack of knowledge." Death cannot overcome knowledge because knowledge is life. So they are opposite to each other. That is, the opposite of life is death, while the opposite of knowledge is ignorance. Let me explain this to you. Behind knowledge is life, or we might say knowledge goes before life. Also, behind ignorance is death, or ignorance goes before death. You must understand that any person flowing in river of ignorance is flowing inside the water of death, although it might not kill immediately. That is why you must always seek and run after knowledge so that you will not be a victim to ignorance.

5.   Goods things never come out of it: No good things come out of ignorance. The only thing it produces is self-satisfaction and pleasure of the flesh which leads to death. The result of ignorance is always bad. Those who are comforted and find pleasure

in ignorance always have a regrettable time in the end or in the future. Ignorance will make you to be behind when others are moving forward and progressing.

6.   Anointing does not kill or stop ignorance: This may confuse you. You may question, "Why can't anointing kill ignorance?" So far the Bible says by the reason of the anointing, all yokes shall be broken (Isa. 10:27). Sure, that is true, but I will explain it better to you. When God anoints you, what the anointing does is to give you the privilege or opportunity to be free from ignorance. It is now left to you to run away from ignorance by seeking knowledge. It can also be explained in this way: the anointing will break the power of ignorance, make the power to be ineffective over you (so that knowledge can have its way into your life if you will allow it), and then give you the opportunity to seek knowledge. Why? Because, life is a matter of choice. God said in Genesis 6:3 that His Spirit shall no longer strife with men. That is, God won't force you or make rival with you, but you are to make your decision or decide what to do when the option has been given to you. Deuteronomy 30:19 says, "I have lay down before you life and death." So, it is now left for you to choose the one you want. But the anointing will always help you to realize what you are doing and correct you from doing wrong things. Although you may still choose to go on your own way, you must understand that God shall surely open doors before you, but it is your responsibility or duty to pass through them, or else, you will remain in bondage despite the open doors. Eventually,

God has already opened doors of greatness to many, but they refuse to move. Let me give you another example: when God created man, the Bible says He blessed them and commanded them to be fruitful. This means God planted you on the surface of the earth so that you can be fruitful. So also, after you have been baptized with the Holy Spirit, you must develop yourself so that you can be fruitful. And Jesus said any tree that does not bear fruit shall be cast into fire (Matt. 3:10, John 15:6, Matt. 25:30). The fruit you are expected to produce is found in the book of Galatians 5:22. That is why God said, His people perish because of lack of knowledge. Note the quote, "His people"; meaning His priest, those who obey Him, the men of God that work in His sanctuary, and those who are called by His name, they perish because of lack of Knowledge. If anointing should kill ignorance, then the priest or people of God will be the most carrier of the knowledge so that ignorance won't be found in them. But the Bible passage tells us here that they are actually the victim of ignorance. Get my point, I am not disputing or neglecting anointing, but what am saying is that anointing helps but does not stop one from making his or her decision. Anointing is like a key or ticket that gives you access to the real knowledge with wisdom and understanding, but it depends on how you make use of it. As a man of God, you must always seek and follow after knowledge if you want your anointing and calling to be effective and to prosper and last long (Mal. 2:7). If anointing kills ignorance, none of ministers of God will end up in hellfire. But there are plenty of those anointed here on earth for the works of God ending up in hell because they permitted ignorance to ruin their life.

7. It cannot withstand knowledge: Knowledge is a light. Darkness cannot stay where light is dominating. When knowledge appears, it will pursue ignorance and render it useless. Ignorance has a great fear for knowledge. That is the reason why it slaughters people before they realize the truth. It knows and understands that when a person allows knowledge into his or her life, it's (ignorance) already in trouble. So it makes every effort to completely blindfold people and lead them to the place of slaughter.

8. Violence is needed to defeat ignorance: You cannot defeat ignorance by gentleness. The only force it respects is violence. When I say violence, I don't mean act of causing trouble or destroying things. No, the violence I'm talking about is great determination, stubbornness, or act to resist nonsense. We can also say holy violence as described in Matthew 11:12, that "And from the days of John the Baptist, the kingdom of heaven suffereth violence and the violent take it by force." Let me explain this to you such that you will understand. It means, since the days of John the Baptist, the kingdom of God (it represents holiness, good place to be, heavenly kingdom, new Jerusalem, and place full of gold and where God lives) suffers violence (permit no nonsense, requires focus act, entails war between good and bad), and it will also take the people who are violent to take it by force. It means to achieve good things in life is not easy. For you to achieve greatness or to be a friend of knowledge, you need violence,

and to be a violent person against ignorance or failure, you still need an extra force, power, and might to achieve the greatness. You can't live like ordinary or common men if you want to be free from ignorance. You must do uncommon things to archive great thing in this life. You need to operate in a special way that will not tolerate any act of nonsense that might want to delay you or stop you. And with this, you will also need to get extra power to move ahead until you get to your Promised Land. May be I should tell you this, good and precious things can only be found in the deep of the sea and not at the top. Jesus told Simon Peter in Luke 5:4 to launch his nets into the deep and let down his nets for a draught. He did not say, spread your net at the top of the sea. You can only find gold, petroleum, etcetera, in the deep and not on the surface. And we only seek after those things (not minding the risk) when we have the knowledge of them. That is why ignorance blinds in order to avoid one from having the knowledge, talk less of pursuing it.

9. It is a waster of resources: Where there is domination of ignorance, there is always wasting of resources. Although God has given all that people or areas need, but because of ignorance, they misuse the gift and grace of God. It is knowledge that makes you know the uses of a thing. It is knowledge that let you know that what you call a waste can be used to make other profitable and essential things. There is no wastage before knowledge. In other words, knowledge does not support wastage but ignorance does.

10. It produces poverty: I will say ignorance goes before poverty. If you are poor, it means you are still ignorant of what you are supposed to know. When you seek knowledge, it will open your eyes to things you are supposed to do to be rich. A community, family, and life will be poor if ignorance is dominating. Ignorance will blind you from seeing the good resources, things, friends, and ideas around. Whereas, these are the things you need for you to excel and prosper in life. I have already told you that ignorance is a killer. You might have everything it takes for you to be rich and still remain poor because of ignorance. Ignorance makes you to be poor in terms of finances, ideas, wealth, education, leadership, health, etcetera. It is when knowledge begins to shine its light that poverty begins to disappear. As long as you are ignorant, you will remain poor. The reason why you experience poverty in any area of your life is because of your level of ignorance and what you are ignorant of may be the most important one that your life needs for prospering. Having money does not make you free from ignorance, and of course, having money is not riches. Understand that.

11. It turns from high to low: Ignorance can make a person fall from grace to grass. When you get to a place by luck or opportune to be in a greater position, your level of ignorance will determine how long you will remain in that position and will also determine whether you will get praise or shame. Opportunities can come at any time; ignorance blinds one from recognizing opportunities. And if you are lucky enough to get

to a position by the opportunity that comes your way, ignorance can bring you down in a moment. It takes much time to build, but it takes little time for ignorance to destroy all that has been built. Anyone who has been captured by ignorance is found to destroy things. And the funniest point is that after destroying, their eyes then open. You may work for twenty years before achieving a success, but ignorance will only help to turn everything back to zero in a twinkle of an eye.

12. It is a killer of destiny: Many destinies have been destroyed because of ignorance. Ignorance has no mercy. Many youths have been destroyed by ignorance. The sad news is that some are still busy celebrating and catching fun in the bosom of ignorance. Many are doing things that are harmful to their life now, but they think they are doing the right thing. Although knowledge surrounds them and keep warning them day and night, they won't listen because they are already a victim of ignorance. Many would have lived to fulfill their destiny and even live longer to eat the fruit of their labor, but ignorance will make them to do what they are not supposed to do at a particular time in their life so that it affects them later. And eventually many have been wasted. It is just like a boy who smoked throughout his early age. Although he was warned by people to stop the act, he did not listen. Even the company that produces the cigarette testifies that all smokers are liable to die young, but still, he did not listen because he has been blinded. Now, his star started shining at his early age and not quite long, ignorance drag him to court of the judgment. He was sick and

was diagnosed of lung cancer, and he eventually died. Answer the question, whose fault is that? Don't you know that this life is based on the principle of sowing and reaping? That is, you sow in every seconds of your life. You can't do without sowing a seed in a day. The seed may be good or bad. And whatever you sow is what you will reap. This is a hard saying. You might not at first understand this, but what you reap in the future will always narrate the stories of your past. For the germination process, first the seed should be sown. Then it should die so that it can germinate, grow, and after some time start producing its fruits. So, ignorance has blinded so many people to do what they are not supposed to do at a particular time so that they can be destroyed later in life. Ignorance has also caused many of forefathers to sow a bad seed in the past for the future generation so that the innocent generation is now reaping the works of the fathers. This is a serious matter. That is why this book is written to deal with the spirit of ignorance in both physical and spiritual manner.

13. It is a man killer disease: Ignorance does not attack animals but man. The reason is that it is a weapon in the hand of the devil. When God created us, He created us in His own image. Not only that, God blessed us and from the beginning of the creation, He made us to rule over all of the creation and even Satan. But the devil deceived man so as to hijack the authority God gave us. The devil made man to sin against God, but nevertheless, there is something that is still in us that is very dangerous to the devil's kingdom. He knows that as soon as our eyes are opened to see these things and we

realize who we truly are, he's already in trouble. That is why he uses ignorance as a weapon to destroy men. Ignorance is a disease to mankind. That is, it is an enemy of man. Once he attacks, his next agenda is to kill, unless it is stopped and cured immediately before it gains more ground on the person. That is why a person who is completely ignorant is in danger and even a disaster to others.

14. It makes generals or high-ranking person to become ordinary: It does not respect dignity. Ignorance does not have respect for your position, level, and achievement. Once you give it a chance, it makes you an ordinary man regardless of your achievements. Many generals or great people became ordinary men because of a mistake they made through ignorance. Examples are Samson and Saul in the Bible. Samson was a great man, but because he was ignorant of the devices of the devil, he became a mere man so that he died with his enemies. Initially, Samson was not an ordinary man who should die a shameful death. He can be likened to an eagle. It is a shameful thing for an eagle to walk with chickens and even die with or like a chicken. Saul disobeyed God because he was ignorant of who God is, and he faced the consequence of disobeying Him. He that prophesied as a prophet before he became a king is now rejected by God and became an ordinary man so that the enemy killed him and took his head away. If you don't mind, I pray that you, as an eagle, will not die as a chicken. If you believe that, say a big Amen.

15. It separates people from God: Ignorance is one of the devices the devil is using to separate people

from God. Many have turned back from serving God because they are ignorant of who God is, and they don't truly understand His work, what He likes and what He hates. Ignorance is one of the ways to deviate from faith. But thank God, because Isaiah 10:27 says, by the anointing, the yokes shall be broken. So it means you can break the yoke off your neck through the power of God. And once the yoke is broken, you must quickly run out finally to seek knowledge. Or else, you will be under the umbrella of ignorance, and it may finally kill you.

16. It proceeds before destruction: As pride goes before destruction, so also ignorance goes before destruction. Whenever ignorance sets in or takes over one's life, its next agenda is to destroy the person. It is just what the Bible says about pride. It is a straight forward statement: when you are ignorant of what pride is and its implications, you will eventually take pride as a normal way of life which will suddenly leads you to destruction. Another good example is the case of the smokers. It is never a hidden truth that the smokers are liable to die young, but ignorance will do a very great job in blindfolding its victims so that they won't even listen to the truth, talk less of choosing the truth. So, when ignorance now finally leads them to the place of destruction, they will then be regretting their deeds which they did in the past. The tragedy of this is that despite many have died because of this mistake, others will not learn because ignorance is dominating their life.

17. Its mission is to steal, kill, and destroy all if possible: Ignorance does not have anything to offer us; its only mission is to destroy all on this

earth if possible. Sometimes, when you don't notice that you're ignorant before it penetrates deeply into your life, it may destroy you in a great way. Many are considering ignorance as their best friend, thinking that, it will help them a lot or it has been helping them. Another tragic thing about ignorance is that once it captures one person, it starts spreading through one person to another. So, if not quickly addressed, it can destroy as many as a community or nation.

18. It produces pride: One of the symptoms of ignorance is pride. People who are proud feel they know all, whereas they knew nothing. Because of this reason, they start behaving as if they are the greatest and may want to be the greatest. Anyone who is proud is completely ignorant. Why? It is because pride goes before destruction and also God hates pride (Prov. 6:16).

19. It can disguise itself as knowledge: Many times, people see ignorance as knowledge. That is the reason why many are victims of ignorance. Once they know something, they don't bother to search or test whether it is truly knowledge or not; however, they accept it and start bragging about it. It is possible to be completely ignorant and yet to the person, he or she is the wisest. These categories of people always believe to be the wisest, to have known all, and they have no need to accept or hear other's ideas or words. The way ignorance appears to be knowledge is like wrapping feces with gold. That is, outwardly, it is gold, but right inside, it is an abomination. When one chooses to keep the wrapped feces, as time goes on, it will begin to decay and cause havoc even to the environment.

20. It turns one to a slave: Ignorance will always make you a slave to a wise person. Maybe I should say that people who are ignorant are always slave to the wise ones. If you decide to remain ignorant, you will surely be controlled by a wise person, no matter the amount of powers you posses. In fact, the power will make you a good slave, whereby you will be dragged and controlled by the wise person with a great force. So, if you decide to fight a wise man with your power, the power will do nothing else than to make you crash terribly. Also, no matter what your age, size, stature, height, complexion, and sex are, you are still a slave to the wise. A good example is an educated man and an illiterate. No matter what the illiterate has or possesses, he is a slave to the educated man, and with the knowledge the educated man has, he can control the illiterate as he wishes.

21. It makes one a vagabond: Being ignorant is like living in the darkness or in a dark world. When you are in the dark, you can't see anyone or any structures and things around. So you begin to walk around without a bearing and focus. And every step you take is likely to land you into a very serious danger. This means, in the dark, there is no hope for surviving, there is no vision of where to go, you can't see anything good, you can be easily ensnared, you only know your mind, and you can't see what's coming your way. The same thing happens when you are ignorant.

22. It cannot be bribed: The only way out or solution to ignorance is knowledge. Any other attempt will surely fail. Money cannot kill ignorance, neither can you bribe it. Bribing in order to escape

ignorance is like pouring water inside a basket. Ignorance won't accept bribe so as to free you. The more you bribe it, the more foolish you become.

23. **Hatred is a product of ignorance:** Another symptom of ignorance is hatred. You can't prove to have knowledge when you neglect love. No matter who you are, if you still have hatred in you, it means you are ignorant. It is a dangerous thing to hate your brother or neighbor. It is certain that before you can hate someone, you would have looked down on the person or made yourself superior to the person. This is pride. Hatred simply means a strong opposition to somebody. The only commandment God gave us in the New Testament was to love our neighbor as our self (Matt. 5:43) and even our enemies (Matt. 5:44). Remember that the Bible says my people perish because of lack of knowledge (Hosea 4:6). You don't know the help the person you hate today will render to you tomorrow. And God can't even forgive or love you because you hate your fellow being. The summary of the truth is that God Himself is Love (1 John 4:16). So when you hate fellow human being whom you see, it is impossible to love God whom you have not seen (1 John 4:20).

24. **It can kill a whole community, nations, and even the world:** Many people, communities, and nations are in bondage now because of ignorance. In fact, a community can be blinded that they won't know right from their left. They won't be able to differentiate what is bad from good. A good way to describe this is a community of people who are illiterate. You must understand that education is not a total solution to ignorance and also

22

education without God only makes one a clever devil.

25. It can appear to be good: Many times, people who are victims of ignorance see it as good thing. They hate knowledge with great passion. Such people always see knowledge as bad and not good thing to have. They always prefer to spend their days and years with ignorance whereby avoiding knowledge.

26. It makes one to die with his or her enemy: Ignorance will always tell you that you can't overcome a circumstance. It will tell you there is no way out unless you kill yourself and die in the circumstance. Any circumstance that seems to be a challenge for you is your enemy which you must conquer. Don't let any circumstance overthrow you. All the days of man are full of evils, risks, and calamities (Job 14:1). But what ignorance does is to let you see it as the end of life, and as a result, it weakens you so that you won't be able to fight the battle before you. Many have committed suicide just because of one circumstance or the other. Ignorance has blinded their sight from seeing themselves victorious in the future. Knowledge will always encourage you in every situation you find yourself and will also provide solutions to every problem. Ignorance will only blind one from knowing the truth that "when there is life, there is hope."

27. It makes one to work like an elephant and eat like an ant: When you work tirelessly without any result, it means you are still ignorant. That is, you are still ignorant of what to do or how to do those things. But you may say, I have sought all possible ways and still they did not yield any

result. Well, the truth of the matter is that for every problem, there are solutions. The reason you don't have good result is that you have not gotten the right knowledge to approach the problem, and this makes you ignorant. I mentioned right knowledge, don't be confused. I told you earlier on that ignorance can disguise itself knowledge and also appear to be good, you remember? So, wrong knowledge is still ignorance. There is no other way to express knowledge than by the name knowledge. When you have not reached hundred percent (perfect), it means you are still below hundred percent. But when you are hundred percent perfect, it means you are. You must always be ready to conquer ignorance in case it wants to approach you again. Ignorance is never tired of enslaving people (it is devil's messenger), so you have to keep on fighting it with the power of knowledge you have.

28. It can be bought: You cannot bribe ignorance, but it can be bought. Ignorance can be bought at both cheap and expensive prices. Many have been enslaved by the ignorance they bought. Example of things people purchased that have made them to be enslaved by ignorance are wrong novels, wrong books, wrong movies, wrong motivational speech, wrong counseling, wrong shows, wrong education, pornography, wrong advice, etcetera. Before you purchase or go for anything, you should seek knowledge to find out what you want to purchase and the implications behind acting on your opinion. Always remember that ignorance is not there to make friend with you but to destroy you, so always resist it, even if it seems attractive.

29. It can be obtained for free: Perhaps, if you don't have enough money to purchase ignorance, you can also have it just for free. That is, you may be given as a gift. That means, before you go after free things or receive free gift, you still need knowledge to know the kind of gift you are given so that you won't receive what will destroy you. Always make sure to get the real knowledge and not fake. Examples of the things obtained for free that enslave people are also the same as the ones mentioned in the previous number (28).

30. It does not cooperate with your destiny or anything good: Ignorance can never cooperate with your destiny; instead it destroys it. That is why, when someone becomes its victim by any means, it always makes the person to regret and be ashamed, and it can go as far by destroying the person.

31. It hates you: Ignorance hates you, and you must also hate it with passion. It is not an enemy you should love because it is not a being like you (flesh) but an evil spirit. This means, it is something you should resist at every seconds of your life.

32. It can take one to hell: It is very possible for one to end up in hell because of ignorance. When you are ignorant of God's word and commandments, it will surely take you to hell. You must diligently seek the knowledge of God. Here, I mentioned God's knowledge, why? The reason is that knowledge comes from God. So the real knowledge or knowledge we are saying is from God. Knowledge of God comes as principles, commandments, and words. All are to give you life because knowledge is life.

33. It is an enemy of knowledge: Ignorance never cooperates with knowledge. They always fight each other. Both are enemies. Ignorance always prevents knowledge from taking over its place. That is why, in many cases, you find it difficult to do good things (things that are beneficial or that will move you forward) but always find it so easy to do things that are unprofitable to your destiny. Take for example, a person who is supposed to read what will be of great benefit to his or her destiny, he or she will always find it difficult to do so, but when it comes to reading rubbish, it is always easy; in fact, he or she can spend much time on them. Why? It is because ignorance will always defend you from reading good books. It uses the power of the flesh. Flesh is yourself and physical part of yourself. So your flesh also can never cooperate with you if you want to achieve success. What the flesh wants is comfort and pleasure. If you want to really make impact or want to acquire knowledge, you must kill your flesh totally. I did not mean that you should kill yourself, but what I mean is that you should discipline and put your flesh (body) under subjection.

34. It cannot build: Ignorance cannot build. When I say build, I mean creativeness and power to build physical and unseen structures. It cannot build anything but rather manipulate, waste, and destroy things that have been built. It is knowledge that makes one to be creative or gives ability to build and not ignorance.

35. It is behind failure: Failure is caused by lack of knowledge. When one fails, it means the person is lacking a particular knowledge. It means you have

not known what you are supposed to know. It does not mean you are completely ignorant. You may be failing because of one thing you need to know that you have not known. Until you get the knowledge needed, success is not guaranteed.

36. It causes sickness: Ignorance has made many to be victims of various sicknesses. Many that are now sick are the real cause of their sickness. Some became victim because of lack of awareness, understanding, and knowledge. Some took drugs they are not supposed to take, some ate what they are not supposed to eat, some drank what they are not supposed to drink, some became addicted to smoking, some did something that was not supposed to be done, and all these are now affecting their lives. It is not all sicknesses that occur naturally, many are caused by us. You can imagine a person who spent all his youthful age smoking. He is now suffering from cancer of the lung at the age of forty-five when he is supposed to start reaping the fruit of his youthful labor and even labor more to enjoy his old age. The sickness eventually killed him. He died because of nothing else but lack of knowledge. You should not live your life anyhow, neither should you do things anyhow. Everything we do now will eventually result in something. You can't do things just for free. What you do now is sow a seed which must be reaped later. It is a must. It is a principle laid down by God. You can't change it. In fact, God did not call us to seek and serve Him in vain (Isa. 45:19). There is a reward for everything done. What you reap depends on the kind of seed you planted or sowed. The truth is that we sow seed or

invest every second of our life. Imagine how many seeds you would have sown in a day, talk less of years. And the day of harvest will surely come. It cannot be avoided. Be mindful of everything you do every second.

37.   It causes untimely death: As I have told you earlier, ignorance kills, and most of the time, it kills at a very young age. It is a must that you should always avoid ignorance. I mean always seek knowledge. Just like what I mentioned in the previous number, many sicknesses killed people at very young age, and most of the sicknesses are caused by the people themselves. Also, most of the seeds sown can get mature and start producing fruit (result or repercussion) at a very short time. As some may take five minutes, thirty minutes, hours, a day, days, months, and years to be ready for harvest, it is possible to start harvesting what we have sown in the past at early stage of our life or of our children and even children's children. What if we have sown a seed that will produce death? Readers, this is the reason why you need to be careful of what you do and always seek knowledge in all aspects of life so that you won't be a victim of ignorance.

38.   It gives room to the enemy: A person who lacks knowledge is never secure. What ignorance do is to open the door widely for the enemy to come in and you may have believed to have gotten adequate security. When you lack knowledge, you will expose your secrets to your enemies. Ignorance will also allow you to open your mouth widely where you are supposed to keep quiet. Talkative are easily ensnared by their words. When you are

ignorant, you will make your enemies your best friends. No one can open the door of your life to enemy if not yourself. A very good example is the story of Samson and Delilah (Judg. 16:1-19). Samson revealed the secrets of his power to Delilah without knowing that Delilah was his enemy and has been sent to pull him down. You must be careful of people you move with and especially the opposite sex. The reason is that most of the time we reveal our secrets to people we move with, and those people may be dangerous to our life and destiny. But knowledge will always let you know the time to speak and to be quiet, who to move with and who to avoid. Sex (the one outside marriage) is a very common tool in which enemies and sickness can enter into one's life. When you have sex with someone, it means you have engaged in a covenant with the person. Through that enemies (spirit and sickness) have a free access to one's life. This is why many are suffering from dangerous and incurable diseases. Don't be ignorant of premarital sex.

39. It generates inferiority: It is ignorance that makes a person to feel inferior to others, neglecting the truth that he or she has been created to be great. God did not create a failure. He has not made you to be inferior to other people. There is something inside of you that is so unique that those people you think are superior to you do not have and the world really has need of it. But instead of working on yourself, you are busy looking at others as special and superior. This is because you lack knowledge. If someone is richer than you, it does not make you inferior to him or her. If he or

she is taller or fatter than you, it does not make you to be inferior to him or her. If he or she is prospering now or in great position, it does not make him or her to be superior to you. You are equal being, and what makes the difference is time and opportunities. Instead of making yourself inferior to people, take and make good use of your time and opportunities.

40. It makes one's life a dumping ground: A dumping ground is a place where wastes are dumped. Waste is an unwanted substance. So also is a person who lacks knowledge. People without knowledge are found of possessing unwanted (not useful) things or ideas. Speech and other things of such people are counted as irrelevant. They always receive wrong and irrelevant information. They are busy bodies. Their ways of life are always irritating. They are always dirty and smelling. They don't have good things in possession. They don't get married to a good person. They are the kind of female that have been randomly sampled by men. They are always hated, and no one wants to move close to them. All these are caused by ignorance.

41. It results to witchcrafts: According to world dictionaries, witchcraft is simply using allegedly magical powers. But, according to God, witchcraft is simply rebellion against God. And God's judgment for such act is death. The Bible says (Exod. 22:18), "Suffered not the witch to live." Disobedience is an act of rebellion. Forming an act of rebellion is as a result of ignorance. When you lack knowledge, you will always be far from the truth. It is when you are ignorant of who God is and His power, you begin to do things that are

against His will. This may bring a great judgment upon your life. No wonder the Bible says, "The fear of the LORD is the beginning of wisdom" (Job 28:28). Those performing witchcraft are always found of destroying, killing, manipulating, lying etcetera. They are traitors. Witchcraft is one of the devices the devil uses to destroy destiny. When you have been enslaved by ignorance, you will be found of performing witchcraft.

42. It can put one in bondage for long: Ignorance doesn't have pity on people. It makes sure he keeps its victim in bondage as long as it could until the person dies or breaks loose. It is possible for one to be enslaved by ignorance for years. Those people are said to be completely ignorant, that is, they grow and live in ignorance every day. It has become their nature.

43. It goes before sin: The reason for sin is lack of knowledge. Knowledge will always give you the awareness of a sin. It will guide you from sinning by telling you the truths. But ignorance will make you to see sin as good thing. Knowledge is a key to righteousness.

44. It is a limitation: Ignorance will always limit you. It will make you to lag behind, to be stagnant, and to go backward. Undeveloped or under develop is as a result of ignorance. Ignorance has limited many community and nations. You will always see those nations or people behind their contemporaries. It will be a very hard thing to find a single development. And if at all there is one, it is always misused or corrupted because ignorance is still in place. People or nation that is developed always seek knowledge and make it their friend.

Remember I told you that education is not the total solution to ignorance. Likewise, knowledge is not limited to education only.

45.	It is a secret agent of death and destruction: Before death and destruction could act, ignorance is always the agent that goes out to make and clear way for them for a good and successful job. Ignorance will prepare its victim for a terrible death and destruction. That is why it is very dangerous to even have pity on ignorance, talk less of accepting it.

46.	It does not respect your personality: It does not matter the kind of person you are, ignorance still remain ignorance. Victims of ignorance are not determined by personality. It does not attack some and leave some, no. Whether you are poor or rich, tall or short, white or black, fat or slim, if you lack knowledge, it means you are ignorant. There are no dignitaries in ignorance. It is just like boarding a plane. You know that there are places for the VIPs, for business, and for the economy in the plane. Maybe during flight, God forbid, if the pilot suddenly announces that the plane is going to crash, I am very sure that the pilot won't tell the passengers that the VIPs will die softly, the business normally, and the economy a terrible death. But they will all experience the same effect without any partiality. Likewise, ignorance does not respect personality.

47.	It does not respect your riches, position, and honor: Just like what I have stated above and earlier, ignorance has nothing to do with your riches and neither can you bribe it. You can be very rich and be completely ignorant. Likewise you can be the most honorable of all and still be ignorant. In fact, ignorance will take advantage of your riches and honor to destroy you on time, because it will produce pride in you, which goes before destruction.

48. It has no respect for age: Many believe that at old age, you will have known all. I tell you, it is very possible for an old person to be completely ignorant. He or she may have lot of experiences and still lack knowledge. There is a saying that experience is the best teacher. It is true, but it is possible to gain more experience without knowledge. The saying simply means one of the best ways to get knowledge is through experience. But the truth is that one can continue having experience without even learning from it. Experience is like a guideline or knowledge to something, and it is never compulsory for one to follow it because life is a matter of choice. Experience or past experiences will tell you how some things were done. It helps you to take caution so that you won't make a mistake. What I am saying is that both old and young people are always victims of ignorance. It is not only the old that are wise and are always full of knowledge. It is ignorance that will make an old person to do abominable things that even the young ones can't do. Also, young people who are supposed to be friends with knowledge are now lacking it. What I am saying is that ignorance won't leave you because you are young or old. Both young and old are found under the canopy of ignorance.

49. It always looks for trouble: One of the fruits of ignorance is trouble. Ignorance never brings peace

but trouble. Ignorance cannot survive where there is peace and can always live long where there is trouble. It is only knowledge that brings peace. You may be confused because you know some people that you believe to be ignorant but are still peaceful. Firstly, remember I told you, ignorance can disguise itself as knowledge. So, what you think is peace is not actually peace. People who are ignorant will always look for trouble either by argument or other means. Peace means freedom, calmness, absence of violence, no disturbances, etcetera. All these cannot be produced by ignorance.

50.   It can be label or tags to one's life: It is very possible for some who lack knowledge to be widely known. It means such people have already been tagged, especially people who are known to be completely ignorant. Mostly, they are tagged because of their blind argument, failure, lack of good ideas, liability, craziness, wrong speech, wrong ideas, dirtiness, and other ways they live their life. Another thing about one who has been tagged with ignorance is that people don't listen to him or her no matter what he or she has to say. And if at all they listen, it is just for them to mock the person.

51.   It brings comfort and not peace: As I have said earlier, ignorance has no peace to offer but calamity, trouble, failure, death, and destruction. What many believe to be peace brought by ignorance is comfort. And the comfort is to prepare its victim for destruction. You can't be comforted and still expect to be a champion. It is during battle that a champion is known and not during comfort. The best ignorance can give

is comfort instead of peace. You must know that comfort will make one lazy, weak, and to do abominable things.

52. It can never bring gain but loss: You will gain nothing if you allow ignorance to dominate your life. Ignorance will always bring loss into one's account. The reason why some people will still be experiencing loss or poverty is that they are still ignorant of some things that should be bringing profit to their accounts. Until they found the knowledge that will show them the solution, ignorance will continue to ruin their accounts. That is the reason why you must seek knowledge before engaging in any business so that you won't come back ruined. When you build or lay your business on ignorance, definitely, the business can't stand. Why? It is because in the course, ignorance would have made you forget some necessary steps and things to apply that will make your business to be rigid and firm. It is like building a house with ordinary sand without cement and concrete. When wind blows over it, it will crumble.

53. It kills potential: Potential means capacity to develop or become something. It is the internal energy that is capable of achieving something or that makes you succeed. But when ignorance dominates, it will kill the potential. It will bring fears to make you to be afraid of success. It will let you do wrong things that are dangerous to your life, health, and destiny. It will make you to always listen to wrong advice that will silence and kill your potential. It will let you to believe what is wrong. You can only build your potential or use your potentials by the help of knowledge.

54. It misuses opportunities: Lots of opportunities have come to some people, but because they are ignorant, they misuse them. Some of the opportunities were lost, and they were never recovered. For you to recognize and make use of opportunities, you need knowledge. Ignorance will always blind you from seeing opportunities. And if at all you see it and have it through the help of knowledge and if you allow ignorance to take over, it will let you hate the knowledge which is still needed to maintain the opportunities. Many would have been great if not for the opportunities they neglected or have misused.

55. It devalues good things: When you are lucky to possess good things, ignorance will find its way to let you rubbish it (if you allow it). Ignorance does not value gold but rather devalue it. Ignorance will make someone to see and use gold as stone. It will disenable one from appreciating precious things. Many, sometimes in one way or the other, are lucky to get things precious or worthy, but because ignorance is in control, it makes them to turn those things that are precious or worthy to an unworthy things. Just like a man or woman who married a woman or man that people believed to be precious. They knew his or her worth is more than rubies and incomparable. But the partner, because he or she is ignorant, will always see the partner as nothing and worthless.

56. It is dirty or behind dirtiness: Dirtiness is as a result of ignorance. The reason why many are dirty is that they don't know the implications of dirtiness and lack the knowledge that could tell them the benefit of cleanliness. As you know,

dirtiness is never a good thing and is harmful to one's life. But people who are dirty are ignorant of this.

57. It is behind corruption: Corruption means immorality, untruthful for personal benefit, rotten, etcetera. The wages of corruption is always terrible. Corruption will always put one to shame, disgrace, reproach, death, hard judgment, curses, and failure. But many are into corruption just because they don't know what it means and its wages.

58. It is behind fraud: Fraud means deception, cheating, and crime. If you take time to study the Bible very well, you will discover that curses are placed on the deceitful or the people who engage in fraud. Especially in Psalm 55:23 where the Bible says, that the bloody and deceitful men shall not live out half their days. That is why you see many people who are fraudulent don't live long. Their end is always terrible. Despite all these consequences of a fraud, many are still or want to be a fraudster because ignorance has blinded them from knowing the truth. Sometimes they may know the truth but don't have the knowledge of the truth.

59. It produces cunning wisdom: To be cunning means to be crafty and deceitful. In a true sense, it means to be performing witchcraft. This means a cunning person is a witch or wizard. So as far as the scripture is concerned, judgment for witchcrafting is death. That means if you happen to be a cunning person, you lack knowledge and moving toward the valley of destruction.

60. It makes one a fool: When you are completely ignorant, and people have known you for that,

people will always count you as a fool. No one will like to listen to you because they believe you to be foolish. Fool means unintelligent, not sensible, and ridiculous.

61. It blinds one: Ignorance will also blind you from seeing things you are supposed to see. Mostly, things that are beneficial to your life will be hidden from you if you allow ignorance to takeover your life.

62. It cannot see far distance or causes short-sightedness: A person who is ignorant can't see far. It means the person can't have a clear vision of the future. They don't have hope, talk less of giving others one. They don't see more than their present place, position, and condition. Such people don't have hope and plans for tomorrow. They can't see beyond their physical life. They can't see great things coming their way. This is caused by ignorance.

63. It makes one to be visionless: Ignorance makes one to be visionless, that is, without potential or foresight for the future. It is related to the one mentioned in the previous number but with some difference. The vision we talk here means future, purpose, and destiny. So, ignorance makes one to be and exist or live without any purpose to fulfill on earth.

64. It can never accept its fault: Its victims can never accept their fault. It will make them to believe they are always right and has no need to be corrected. You can't see people of such saying sorry. It is an abomination for them to accept their fault. Proving them wrong will always lead to a great argument and later cause conflict.

65. It always looks for excuses: When you are the kind that like giving excuses, you are ignorant. An excuse is different from a reason. Excuses are things spoken for justification, for release from obligation. It also means wrong reason; while a reason is a cause for doing something. There is no excuse for any failure, but there are always reasons for failure. Excuses are products or symptoms of ignorance.

66. It is a liar: Ignorance is never truthful. It is a liar. In many ways, ignorance will tell you that what is bad is good, what is wrong is right, bondage is freedom, comfort is peace, and darkness is light. Ignorance will always speak contrary to the truth. There is no truth in it, because it works with the devil which is known to be the father of lie. If you always lie, you lack knowledge. Or if you see someone who always lies and he or she is known for it, then you should understand that he or she is an ignorant person.

67. It has enticing word to capture its victim: It is sometimes easy to be victim to ignorance because it mostly captures its people through enticement and deceptive words. But once you have knowledge, you will always know the deception of ignorance.

68. It is always found in the company of fools: If you want to know what and who ignorance really is, how it acts, and to get enough description about it, you just need to locate the company of fools and you will have a lot to get. Ignorance cannot survive in the company of the wise because they always seek after knowledge. The best habitation for ignorance is the bosom of a fool. When you see

a fool, you have just seen ignorance at work. If you are able to recognize a fool, you will know what and who ignorance is and can say lot about it.

69. It is a failure called success: When ignorance succeeds in blinding people, they will see it as a success instead of a failure. They will always like to embrace it rather than rejecting it. Ignorance is deceitful.

70. It is bondage called freedom: It is just like what I said in the previous number. People who have been blinded by ignorance will always see ignorance as freedom rather than bondage.

71. It causes madness and craziness of the mind and brain: Madness means psychiatric disorder. To be mad means to have psychiatric disorderliness, to be angry, and to be rash, passionate, and widely excited. Ignorance can make one to have internal disorderliness. Such people will always get angry at the slightest provocation, show interest in wrong and bad things, aggressive, hate people without cause and always curse without a cause. These are internal madness or disorderliness because all these things cannot be found in a normal person (wise or knowledgeable person).

72. It's always willing to die for everything: Ignorance always makes people to die for everything. Its victim doesn't have an immune against death of any kind. They don't know what death is and what happens after death. They don't understand that others will continue to live after they die. In many cases, we have seen or heard of people who died for the freedom of their people or nation, and some died to create great things. But ignorant people will always wish to die for unreasonable

things. Unreasonable things that their people can't even benefit after their death. They always wish themselves dead for any little challenge. A very good example is a girl of about eighteen years who decided to kill herself because a boy has just broken her heart. She killed herself because she lacked knowledge. Some even killed themselves because someone disgraced them, they failed a particular thing, or they are jilted or cheated. All these are due to ignorance.

73.   It always falls for everything: Ignorance will make one to always fall for everything. They won't be able to stand for long but always fall by little touch, trouble, and challenges. It also means their heart is easily broken and they get tired of situations, get discouraged at easy effect, get burned up at a very low temperature, get affected by little circumstances, take challenges as dangers, give up easily, and always regret themselves ever being born or alive. Ignorance causes people to do all these. They don't know that where there is life, there is hope. They don't know that flies will only surround a shining light and not the dead ones. This means the challenges you faced shows that there is something great in you that must be established.

74.   It makes knowledge to be too expensive: Ignorance let people see knowledge as something too expensive to get. It always discourages people from seeking or accepting knowledge because it is never in good terms with knowledge (they are enemies). Its victim always sees knowledge as things which must be pursued with billions in the pocket. It lets people see knowledge as something that cannot be obtained without passing through fire. If you really

want to survive or live long, you need to kill your ignorance. You must make it to be functionless in your life.

75. It gives wrong understanding: It always gives wrong understanding of knowledge or something. When you are told something or you got a particular knowledge, ignorance will make you to get wrong understanding of such thing. People who have been captured by ignorance always get miss-quoted words. When you tell them something, they will always get the wrong understanding of what you told them.

76. It generates false doctrine in the church of God: It is a tragedy that many so-called ministers of God have allowed ignorance to eat them up. They reject knowledge as spoken by God in Hosea 4:6. And as result of that, they bring false doctrine to God's people because ignorance has made them to get the Word of God wrongly. If you want to succeed in the ministry of faith, you need to hate ignorance by seeking and going for knowledge always. Ignorance is a very great device in the hand of the devil to capture most ministers of God. The devil knows very clearly that when you lack knowledge, your fear for God will reduce, you will be prayerless, and even God rejects such people as it was stated in Hosea 4:6.

77. Indiscipline is a product of ignorance: Ignorance makes one to be rude and indiscipline. Indiscipline means lack of control. Meaning, such victim won't be able to caution his or herself because he or she did not know the dangers behind it. Such people do things the way they feel, act the way they like, speak the way they like, and always disobey.

78.   It makes one to be an abomination: When a person is completely ignorant, it tagged the person as an abomination. It will make the person to be horrible and shameful and make people to dislike the person. People will always flee from the person. No one will want to see such person around. Ignorance is a spirit that must be ejected out of one's life.

79.   It causes spiritual deafness and blindness: Ignorance disconnects one from God, and as a result, the person won't be able to hear or see spiritual things. If such person has been hearing God before and see things maybe in dream, he will no longer hear and see because ignorance has taken over him or her.

80.   It is behind selfishness: Ignorance keeps people from giving. It disallows them from knowing the profit of giving. It makes them to see giving as wasting or losing. And if at all they will give, they will always give out to things that are useless and unprofitable. Every selfish person lacks knowledge because they did not know that when they give out, they will surely receive the multiple portion of what they have given. It is only knowledge that can let you know the secrets of giving. Giving is an investment.

81.   It is behind spiritual dirtiness: That is, it is behind sin. Ignorance is what is making people to sin. Had it been they have the knowledge that will tell them the truth, they won't have gone to sin. But because they don't know the consequences of sins, they keep on enjoying their sinful life without caring about what they will face after they die. Many times, they would have listened to preachers, telling them to repent, but unfortunately,

ignorance has made them blind. No wonder our reference passage says, "My people are destroyed because of lack of knowledge" (Hosea 4:6).

82.   It is behind idolatry: Why will you worship a god that cannot talk, speak, and save? This is a great ignorance. Ignorance makes people to serve idols (Isa. 45:20). Idols may not necessarily be a carved image. An idol is anything that you exhort or worship instead of the Living God. It is anything that takes the place of God in your life. It is anything that you love more than God. The wrath of God is always upon those people. As far as the scripture is concerned, an idol can be gold that you are wearing, your children, money, material things, etcetera.

83.   It produces wrath: Wrath means great anger. Ignorance makes people to exhibit great anger without any or little provocation. They destroy everything around them whenever they exhibit their wrath. They even injure themselves during the cause. Every little situations or provocation generate wrath in them. They get wrath without a cause. Their eyes may eventually open after they have destroyed all. This is a great disease caused by ignorance and must be cured before it destroys one's life.

84.   It produces envy: Ignorant people always envy others. To envy means to want what somebody else has. And by so doing you start comparing yourself with them. The Bible says that those who compare themselves with others are not wise (2 Cor. 10:12). And when you are not wise, it means you lack knowledge. Ignorance will make you to look at people's life to live yours. Then, you now begin

to live a duplicate life. It will make you to neglect your original (your real self). If you always envy others, it means you are ignorant.

85.   It is behind faith without work: Ignorance will let someone to have a fruitless faith. The Bible recommends that every faith must be back up with work. It means faith without work is dead (James 2:20). Every faith without work is an imagination or dreams that can never come to pass. It means building castle on the air or thinking of impossibility or fantasy. That is the principle for faith. You must understand that. Some can spend hours praying for riches without ready to work. Don't be deceived. God is not mocked (Gal. 6:7). Whatever you are facing does not change God. The Bible says, He is the same yesterday, today and forever (Heb. 13:8). When Jesus wanted to feed the five thousand men, He multiplied the little that was available. That is what faith does. When you dispense little energy without being lazy, then God will bless and multiply your little effort to yield you great reward. You must understand the principles of God. He wants you to take steps, and then He will help you. God won't do for you what you can do. He does what is impossible or too hard for you to do because He is God of possibility. Stop praying a fruitless prayer and stop mocking yourself.

86.   It produces laziness: A lazy person lacks knowledge. God does not tolerate laziness. A lazy person can't walk with God. Ignorance makes people to hate work. It always makes one to be at comfort all the time. Meanwhile, comfort is dangerous. Comfort means to rest or relax. Is it possible to relax in the centre of a battle? This life

is an endless battle. Every one born to this life must fight till he or she dies. So there is no room for laziness in the battle of life. You can't be free from battles while still alive, because it is endless. The battles of life have stages or levels; every stage or level you are able to conquer promotes you to the next serious level. That is, the higher you go, the tougher it becomes. Those who have conquered one level or the others are the ones making impact in the world. Unfortunately for them, the battle continues till they die. That is why laziness is a dangerous act to perform so that you won't be defeated in the battle of life.

87. It provokes: Ignorance will make you to always provoke people. People are provoked by what you say, what you do, and the way you are living your life. Your words provoke them because you don't talk with knowledge. What you do is rubbish to them and your way of life does not make meaning to them. The dangerous thing is that you might even be provoking someone who has been destined by God to be your ladder to the mountain or land of fulfillment.

88. It desires vain glory: Vain means unsuccessful, very proud, useless, and empty. Glory means praises, achievement, awesome splendor, and exaltation. What ignorance does is to let one to always long for empty achievements or praises, that is, useless praises. Ignorance always makes people to seek after the praise of men. They always wanted to be praised for every little thing they did and useless things done.

89. It is not ready to fulfill purpose: Ignorance makes people to neglect their purpose on earth but

rather running after its pleasures. People who are ignorant do not believe in destiny or purpose. They have a strong belief in fate. They are not ready to impact life but always want to benefit from it. They have sold their birthright, destiny, and talent for a token.

90.   It perishes at last: As you know from our reference passage in the Bible, ignorance perishes. That is, people perish because of lack of knowledge. Ignorance always crash down its victim. That is why I said earlier that it destroys in a very hard way. Perish means completely destroyed or disappear. Ignorance has succeeded in destroying people.

91.   It does not respect your achievements: No matter what you have achieved in the past, you can still be a victim of ignorance. Your achievement might prove that you have been able to overcome ignorance in some areas, but it does not mean that you can never be a victim. Battle with ignorance is a continuous battle. When you conquer one, you then get ready for a greater or harder one.

92.   It produces fear: Fear has been the reason why many are failing in life. It is either the fear to live, to succeed, or to be great. The Bible says that God has not given us the spirit of fear, but of power, of love, and of a sound mind (2 Tim. 1:7). This means, fear is never from God and that he did not create us with fear. Fear is a feeling produced as a result of ignorance. Many are afraid of one thing or the other just because they are ignorant of what such thing is and who they really are. You don't need to fear failure, poverty, sorrow, etcetera. They are not your portion. God did not create

them with you, so you should be confident that you will overcome them no matter how strong they are. You can't defeat a giant or strong man with fear, but you can be destroyed as result of fear in you. Little fear in your life is enough for enemies or situations to conquer you. You need to get the knowledge in order to overcome fear. It is because ignorance will always lead you to even fear a cockroach.

93. It is the greatest enemy of mankind: Ignorance does not wish the existence of mankind. It is like the devil. As I have told you earlier, it hates mankind with passion. The Bible says God's people are destroyed because of ignorance. And you know that destruction is different from ordinary death. Destruction means thorough damage, unrepairable, and beyond measure. But it is sad that as bad or as destructive as ignorance is, it still has many followers than knowledge and many are still willing to dwell in its bosom for the remaining days of their life.

94. It does not care about the amount of lives it wastes per day: Ignorance does not pity life nor does it pity the number of lives it wasted per day. Wasting about million souls or lives today doesn't mean he can't do more than that tomorrow. Wasting lives is its work that must be done. It has no other mission than that. It is now left to you to choose for yourself what you wish. Either you wish to be its victim or friend of knowledge.

95. It is a thief: The greatest thief is not your neighbor or enemy, but the devil that uses ignorance to steal what belongs to people. Any little chance you give ignorance in your life is enough for it to

steal half of your life. It does not waste time. It is not a fool; it knows what it's doing. It is us that we don't know what we are doing. And when you give it a chance to steal, it does not steal little. It is like giving it a blank check, and it does not enter small amount but a very big and if possible all the deposit in your account at that single opportunity you give it. You need to avoid ignorance violently.

96. It puts one in danger: An ignorant person is always in danger of what will happen next. Why? It is because there is no security in ignorance. I have already told you that ignorance is a darkness or veil that puts one in darkness. As long as you are without light that could help you see what's around you, you will be in a serious danger because you can be attacked by anything.

97. Ignorance does not respect dignity: Ignorance does not respect who you are just as I have mentioned earlier on. The respect you deserve in the community is not something for it to consider. In fact, it makes use of your dignity to disgrace you in public and destroy you terribly. That is why you see that dignitaries who are ignorant are always falling terribly. And the devil will even go as far to help you publicize what has happen to you so that you are not covered. That is why, I would advise you that before you go for a leadership post or any post that can make you a dignitary, you should make knowledge your best friend. Or else, you will only dig a very big hole in distance by making ignorance your friend.

98. It causes weakness: One of the symptoms of ignorance is weakness. This means physical, spiritual, emotional, creativeness, and mental weakness. The

simple reason for this is that you've not obtained the knowledge that will make you strong. In other words, you are ignorant of what to do to overcome the weakness.

99. Ignorance does not respect leadership: Ignorance does not respect a leadership position. Instead, it makes use of leadership positions to capture and destroy more people. It knows very well that once it succeeds in capturing the leaders, then to destroy him and his followers will be an easy job. What about if the leader has thousands of followers? That is why you see many leaders feeding their own people to lion. Many people would have lived long and be successful if only they have a good or wise leader. Any leader who lacks knowledge is destruction to his people. We need to choose our leaders rightly, and if it has been chosen, we need to protest. Bad leader will always produce a bad fruit. The Bible says, smite the shepherd, and the sheep shall be scattered (Zech. 13:7; Matt. 26:31; Mark 14:27).

100. Ignorance is not lack of money: Although you lacking money may be as a result of your ignorance, ignorance goes beyond lack of money. You can be rich and still be ignorant.

101. Ignorant is not low age: You are not ignorant because you are small in age. Although it is true, ignorance is more than that. You may be seventeen years old and be a teacher to fifty-year-old man. The Bible makes us to understand that at the age of twelve years, Jesus started listening and asking questions to the Pharisee or elders in temple that they marvel of the kind of person He is (Luke 2:46). Age is not a barrier for ignorance.

102. Ignorance is not lack of power: Although one of the effects of ignorance is lack of power, it is not always true in all cases because ignorance goes beyond that. Bible says wisdom is better than weapon of war (Eccles. 9:18). It means you can be powerful and still be ignorant. However, with knowledge, you can defeat the person who claims to be powerful.

103. Ignorance is not mute, or not talking: You are not ignorant because you are not speaking. In fact, the best way to know a wise person is when he or she is slow to speak and fast to hear and understand. (James 1:19)

104. Ignorant is not gentleness: Because you are gentle doesn't mean you are ignorant. Knowledge is not violence. It is ignorance that is a trouble maker as I have said earlier on. Knowledge is a peacemaker.

105. Ignorance does not respect your calling: If you have the highest anointing or calling and you don't flee and wage war against ignorance, it will later destroy you despite all the anointing. God says, His people are destroyed because of ignorance (Hosea 4:6). He means His people, and when you read further, He said he will reject His priest because they rejected knowledge. Moses as powerful as he was could not reach the Promised Land because of lack of knowledge. He disobeyed God's commandment when he smote the rock twice when God instructed him to smite once (Num. 20:11). He later realized in Deuteronomy 32:31 that God himself is the Rock of ages and he said "for their rock is not as our Rock . . ." Knowledge brings good character. And when you have bad character, you are already finished no

matter in which position you are and how much amount of anointing is there on you or what your calling is.

106. Ignorance lacks respect: I have already said that. But in addition, people who are ignorant don't have respect for others. They are always rude. They find it difficult to respect elders, authorities, and dignitaries. They are not submissive. And to worsen their case, they don't even respect God nor do they fear Him. You should flee from such people so that they won't implicate you.

107. Ignorant is equivalent to foolishness: Other name ascribed to a person who is completely ignorant is fool. And if there is better, greater, or worse name to give them, we can say they are.

108. Ignorance is a deadly poison: Ignorance is a deadly poison that those who have ever drunk it don't escape death and destruction unless it is quickly treated by knowledge which has power over it.

109. Ignorance kills opportunities for a greater level or chance: Many people who are supposed to have gotten promotion to a higher level in life, their career, education, and destiny missed the opportunities because of ignorance. People lose chances because of ignorance. Ignorance can make you misbehave to the person who is supposed to promote you and take you to the next level. The children of Israel provoked God in the wilderness that God has to swear by Himself that none of them from twenty years upward will enter the Promised Land (Num. 14:28). They said God cannot deliver them from the giant men of Amalekites because they have been captured by ignorance.

110. Ignorance makes a son to become a bastard: A son is supposed to be in charge of his father's properties and inherit them. But ignorance will make a son to become a bastard. Because of ignorance, he will misbehave so that his father gives him no access to his properties. A bastard does not have an inheritance. That is how some are to God. They don't receive from God because they are bastard. Although they are created by God, they have sold themselves to the devil, making themselves a child of the devil. They now behave like their father (the devil) and have to inherit what belongs to him which is the hellfire. But sons and daughters of God always receive things from God when asked and will surely inherit His kingdom.

111. Ignorance create loophole to one's life: Ignorance creates a loophole into one's life, that is, ignorance will give room to all kinds of things including one's enemies. It will make one's life to be available to all kind of things that can destroy.

112. It is very possible to become a professor and still be a fool: It is very possible to have acquired all knowledge that one is called a professor and still be foolish. When you get disguised knowledge or counterfeit knowledge, you are still a fool, no matter what your level is. It is very easy to identify such people. Just take a look into their way of life, what they do, and what they say. Then it tells you whether they are truly wise or foolish.

113. Your environment determines your level of ignorance but may not conclude on your state of ignorance: Where you come from and the place you are living can tell maybe you are ignorant

or not. Although some time, it is not always 100 percent true, but at least 80 percent because where you come from and where you are living determines your life and destiny. Nevertheless, living in an environment dominated by ignorance or coming from such place doesn't mean you should be ignorant for life. You can make a difference because knowledge is always there to help you out. Because your family is known for failure does not conclude that you will fail in life. If you want, you can change your family's history. Only seek knowledge to get the right procedure or what to do so that you can be free.

114. Your parent or family determines your level of ignorance: Since you are brought up by your parent, you learned what you now know from them. They taught you most of the things you know. Definitely, if they are completely ignorant, you are also ignorant because they pass it to you or taught you that same ignorance. And if your parent is otherwise, then you are. Although you can determine to get out of ignorance, your parent or family determines at most or least 90 percent of your character. This is because you grow up there, you are biologically connected, and you have the same way of life.

115. Your belief determines your level of ignorance: What you believe determines your level of ignorance because what you believe will determine your life and character. If you believe a wrong thing, you will always live a wrong life. You are what you believe.

116. Ignorance can put a whole nation in bondage: It does not mind putting a whole nation in bondage.

In fact, we can mention many nations which are under the bondage of ignorance now. When you study such nations, you will discover some of the symptoms of ignorance mentioned in this book. Many nations would have grown if not for the ignorance caging them.

117. Ignorance can put a whole family in bondage: It is very possible for a family to be under the bondage of ignorance. Just as we mention many symptoms and truths about ignorance, you can take a look at your family whether your family is a victim. You can then seek knowledge to tell you the right steps to take in order to be free from ignorance.

118. Ignorance can be passed from one generation to another: If it is not quickly addressed, it can pass from one generation to another whereby forming a trend. It can form a trait.

119. It can be passed from one person to another: If you are friend with an ignorant person, you can also be initiated by this ignorance. There is a saying that you show me your friend and I will tell you who you are. It can spread through people.

120. It is always against the truth: Ignorance is not always in terms with the truth. It is always at war with truth. One of the ways its victim is known is that they get angry when they are being told the truth. They don't like to hear the truth. They hate truth. You can't see such people going for the truth but instead for lies and love doing wicked things that are against the truth.

CHAPTER FOUR

WEAPONS OF IGNORANCE

We've understood that ignorance is on assignment to destroy human beings. Let us now look at the weapons used by it to destroy people. We will look at it one by one so that you won't fall into its bondage, and if you have fallen, then it will help you to know your weakness and the loophole or what is causing ignorance to rule over you.

1. Laziness: Many are so lazy to seek knowledge. Before ignorance could capture one, it uses laziness to hinder the person from learning or seeking what is good. It knows that knowledge does not tolerate laziness. As a matter of truth, a lazy person should not expect knowledge to live with him or her. When you allow laziness to rule over you, you have just signed a dangerous contract with ignorance. A lazy person cannot get knowledge nor can he or she work with it. Laziness goes before failure. The common reason why many are failing in different aspects of life is because they are lazy. They are neither ready to work nor ready to take a step. They always want cheap result. They love shortcut not knowing that shortcut is a dangerous cut. In fact, God don't take His own people through a shortcut whenever He is leading them to their place of destiny. God leads the children

of Israel through the wilderness (long cut) to train them and to help them get rid of their rubbish. (Make sure you get our next book titled Get Rid of Your Rubbish). Anything you get cheaply may not last long and may contain deadly poison that can harm. Man's labor is a commandant from God to satisfy him. He then promises to bless our labor so that small work with diligence will yield much profit. You can never be satisfied with another man's labor. Another man's sweat is a poison to your body unless God gives you. (Because He owns all things and gives it to whoever He wishes. Eccles. 2:26, Isa. 45:14). So, when laziness comes in, ignorance follows. Always take note of any weakness in you to avoid laziness.

2.   Blindness: I did not mean physical blindness. I mean blindness in terms of insight, foresight, spiritual, intellectual, and vision. Blindness is a very good tool in the hand of ignorance. Once it blinds you from seeing the truth, you are finished. Anytime it wants to capture its victim, it makes sure it blinds them so that they won't see true knowledge that will deliver them. Remember, I told you that ignorance is a spirit? Ignorance makes use of blindness to cover one's face from seeing the knowledge. Although knowledge lives with you, is close to you, speaks to you, wants to save you, you won't even recognize it, talk less of allowing it to save you from the power of ignorance. These are the ways it appears in our physical life, that is, the ways blindness affect us physically; it makes one not to see what will be useful to him or her, it separates one from good friend, it makes you to see bad things as good

and good as bad, it kills one's understanding so that the person will not understand the word of knowledge spoken to him or her, it disallows one's brain from thinking right, it makes one to transgress against law or commit an offence, and the person's eyes will become open after his deeds so that he starts to blame himself for doing such things.

3.   Pride: Pride is also a weapon that ignorance uses to capture its victim. When you start feeling self-satisfaction or exhorting yourself or feeling superior, it shows that ignorance is already destroying you. The Bible says "pride goes before destruction (Prov. 16:18, Prov. 13:10). Ignorance can't work in someone's life without using all these weapons. The devil understands the Bible even more than many of us. He knows that God hates the proud look. What causes the downfall of the devil? It is pride. In other words, for him to destroy mankind, he makes use of ignorance to attack man with pride. The angel of the Lord destroyed Herod because he did not give glory to God (Acts 12:19-23). He did not put his pride under subjection when his people were praising him. You should be careful when people praise you because ignorance do take the chance to destroy people whereby producing pride in them. Knowledge will tell you to always avoid such things or flee from it. It is a dangerous thing to be ignorant of all these things. A proud person is a fool despite all the achievements. In fact, God himself destroys such people.

4.   Believing to have known all: That is a breaking point for ignorance to execute judgment on people. This is

a complete ignorance. It is very difficult to save such people. Ignorance gradually drags such with the mindset (believing to have known all) to a place of destruction. Ignorance combines this weapon with pride and blindness to totally destroy people. Check yourself, did you always feel to have known all in such a way that you don't listen to correction or don't want to listen to ideas of others? Because it is only the dead that don't learn or have no need to learn again. Examine yourself to know where you belong. You can be saved if you accept your fault. Whenever a mad or crazy person realize that he or she is, there is 99 percent hope of total recovery.

5. Illiteracy: This is also one of the weapons ignorance use to put people under bondage. Illiterate means uneducated and unable to read or write. A person without education can't flow or prosper as much and will even find it difficult to fulfill his or her purpose. It (illiteracy) affects a person's thinking and other way of life. This is a great ignorance. How will you read what is hidden in paper? And how will you write to hide things in paper if you are illiterate? It affects people's communication. Such people in this category are easily destroyed, and sometimes they destroy themselves for lack of education. Education helps to develop your talents and skills. It helps you to know what is good and what is right. It develops your thinking. It enhances sharp sense. It helps in communication. It is a tool of knowledge. It distinguishes you. It gives you honor. That is why people say education is the best legacy.

6. Money and riches: Money, riches, and wealth are parts of weapons ignorance uses to deceive

people into destruction. Ignorance makes use of money to allow them get carried away and generate pride in them. Money is a weapon of destruction if not carefully handled. Many have been destroyed because of money. Money goes a long way that the Bible says money is the roots of all evil (1 Tim. 6:10). That is why God blesses His people rather than giving them money or riches. When God blesses you, you will not lack anything needful. You will always be satisfied with what you have and enjoy peace in all areas of life. But money can't buy peace, life, sleep, and lot more. Bible says God gives the sinner the work of gathering (Eccles. 2:26). This means heaping up riches is a work of gathering which the sinners do. I am not saying you should be poor. But don't put your trust in money or riches. Ignorance has succeeded in destroying many people because of their riches. It is true that money answered all things without excluding destruction. Money also buys destruction or says yes to destruction. When destruction or ignorance requested for candidates to be slaughtered, with the help of money or riches, one may be qualified or available for it. That is why Jesus says it will be very difficult for the rich to enter the kingdom of God (Luke 18:24). It is not that money is not good but it has made them to forget God and many are being controlled by it. When ignorance uses riches against one, it also combines blindness and pride so as to destroy its victim terribly.

7.   Ungodliness: Ignorance draws people away from God, in other words, to destroy their lives. If you are godly, you will be devoted to the things of

God and will always want to be in His presence. However, ignorance produces ungodliness so that one won't even be in the presence of God, talk less of getting the knowledge. An ungodly person is a wicked person and the Bible says God is angry with the wicked everyday (Ps. 7:11). God Himself destroys the wicked (Ps. 9:5). That is why you must search and examine yourself very well. This is the truth I must tell you. When you know the truth, then, it will set you free (John 8:32).

8.   Lies: If you are a liar, you are ignorant. You may think you are smart. The truth is that telling lies makes you a fool. The end of all liars is destruction (Rev. 21:8). Whether you like it or not and whether you believe it or not, that is the truth. Liars are deceptive people. Deception destroys. That is why it is a weapon in the hands of ignorance to carry out the devil's assignment. You can't be a liar and expect a true prosperity because the sword is always upon the liars (Jer. 50:36). What sword does is to slay. Anything you achieve through lies will only trouble or destroy you in the end. These are what ignorance does to destroy mankind. And these are the truths that many people don't know. Many liars count it as a normal thing to lie, not knowing that ignorance is at work consuming them gradually so that they perish. I have told you that ignorance is a spirit in mission to destroy. It uses lie as one of the weapons to carry out its mission.

9.   Unfaithfulness: When you cannot be trusted, it means you are under the umbrella of ignorance. You need to examine yourself. Unfaithfulness is weapon of destruction. Having confidence

in an unfaithful man in time of trouble is like a broken tooth and a foot out of joint (Prov. 25:19). An unfaithful person is always rejected and even doomed to destruction. Unfaithfulness closes doors of opportunities. Unfaithful person is a liability and does nothing than to bring losses to one's accounts or life. People always run away from such people. Ignorance uses unfaithfulness and has succeeded in destroying many. When you are unfaithful in little things, then many things cannot be entrusted to your hands (Luke 16:11-12). When you notice a trace of unfaithful in you, be alert that it is ignorance at work and on mission to destroy you.

10. Carelessness: It is the opposite of diligence. If you are careless, you should be expecting failure. Carelessness will always make one a fool. It separates one from knowledge. It makes one to be losing rather than gaining. A careless person can't get knowledge because he or she won't seek it. It is a weapon of ignorance that causes failure and destruction.

11. Anger: Human's anger is next to madness. Anger is an agent of destruction. It opens one's life for destruction. Anger can be expressed in positive and in negative manners. Expressing anger in a positive way is like rebuking in love, saying no to ignorance, having displeasure for failure and poverty, getting angry to overcome a terrible situation, and praying with passion (that is, desperate prayer from the depth of your heart). Expression of anger in a negative manner is anger without a cause, destroying things, anger against righteousness or good things, wrath to

destroy fellow brethren, and keeping malice and hot-tempered with small provocation. Angers of man does not produce godliness but only stir up strife (Prov. 15:18). Anger is an enemy of good things. Ignorance provokes anger in one for swift destruction. Ignorance makes it impossible to control one's anger. If you get angry easily, you should be aware that you are ignorant and ending toward destruction. Don't be a friend to an angry person because he or she may harm, kill, and destroy at a very slight provocation. Be careful not to work and have business with an angry man, because it will only take him few minutes to destroy what you have being building for years. Don't marry an angry man or woman; he or she will always threaten you with his or her anger. Avoid provoking an angry man or woman; he or she can destroy at a little provocation. If you are the type that gets angry easily, seek knowledge to help you out.

12. Weakness in learning: Ignorance makes people to be weak when it comes to learning. One of the ways to acquire knowledge is by learning. Learning has always been the secret of a good leader. There is a saying that readers are leaders, but to be honest with you, it is never so in many cases. I will say learners are leaders. A reader can only be a leader if he is learning from what he's reading. It is possible to be reading to have a fun and excitement. Anyway, you can also learn when you read rubbish. That is, you learn to do or practice the rubbish you read. You are trained to be a leader and not read to be leader. A reader is not capable of being a leader but a learner. You don't read to

drive but learn to drive. It is what you learn that determines your capacity and immune against ignorance. Ignorance creates a weakness in people to guide them from learning what will profit them and that will make them to escape its capture. A learner is not easily captured by ignorance because he is a friend of knowledge. Learners are threat to ignorance. A child or babies don't read to walk or talk, but learn. It is wrong saying that a reader is a leader. It is only reader who learns when reading is a leader. When you notice that you get weak when it comes to learning, you should be aware that ignorance is at work to destroy you. You must learn to overcome failure in all forms of professions.

13. Wrong belief: Ignorance has succeeded in feeding people with wrong belief. It makes them to always believe wrong things so that it prevents them from having knowledge. When you are lost, you are likely to be destroyed. It uses wrong people, wrong pastor or ministers, wrong leaders, and wrong family and relatives to make one believe what is wrong. When you don't believe what is right, you are very near to destruction and life is not guaranteed. What you believe will determine your life and how far you will go in life. What you believe controls your life. That is why you need to seek knowledge of the truth.

14. Wrong information: Information prepares you. Good information prepares you for success, while wrong ones prepare you for destruction. When you are not properly informed, you cannot be properly prepared. The type and kind of information you get determines the kind of life you will live, your

security, and your tomorrow. Wrong information creates a platform for failure and destruction. When you get wrong information, it will strengthen ignorance or create a good platform for ignorance to rule you. Wrong information sometimes comes as knowledge. That is why you need wisdom to discern ignorance from knowledge and wrong from good. Knowledge is behind good information, while ignorance is behind wrong information.

15. Partnership with unwise friends: Keeping company with fools will only aid one's destruction. Your friend determines or shows who you are. The company you move with have a lot to say about your life. As a matter of truth, company with fools corrupt good manners (1 Cor. 15:33). Ignorance connects you with fools so that you won't escape its terror. When you move with unwise people, it strengthens ignorance over your life. It is a lie to say you don't know whether your friends are wise or not. Well, you don't know because you are alike or you both are blind. However, the people around will always tell you. Unwise people have many characters, but what you should understand is that all their characters are not good. Not even one. Their deeds are always corrupt. Now, you should be able to recognize them. As soon as you understand this, don't hesitate to flee from them. Come out and separate yourself from them (2 Cor. 6:17).

16. Talkativeness: Those who keep their mouth and their tongue keep their soul from troubles (Prov. 21:23, Prov. 13:3). When you talk too much, you are exposing yourself to serious destruction. Bible refers to those people as busybodies (2 Thess.

3:11, 1 Tim. 5:13). During the course of excessive talking, you speak out your life and your secrets to the enemies. You even slandered people by your talkativeness. This is none other than ignorance. It is ignorance that makes people to speak what they are not supposed to even speak out. When you guide your tongue and mouth, you preserve your life from destruction (1 Peter 3:10, Prov. 21:23). Your level of talkativeness will determine your level of destruction. Talkativeness that I'm talking about is talking excessively, including rubbish that is not supposed to come out of your mouth. Talkativeness will always open one's life to dangers.

17. Envy: When you envy people, it shows that you are not contended with what you are having. And by this, strife and grievance come which will put your life in serious danger. It is ignorance that makes people to envy others so as to create a room for destruction in their life. You don't need to envy what people have. Be satisfied with what you have because you don't know their source of getting such things. Instead of envying people, you can desire or appreciate what they have. You can then try to get your own. But if you are unable to get yours, check and examine yourself to know where you are failing and lacking so as to correct yourself. Or let me say, instead of longing or desiring what others have, desire something greater because what they have is not the greatest of its kind. When you pursue something higher and greater, you will make a difference. Getting common things with others make no difference out of you. It doesn't make you to be distinct.

Don't envy people, but focus on your own gift, talent, and ability that will give you something better.

18. Fornication and adultery: These are mighty weapons in the hands of ignorance through the devil to destroy people. Ignorance has blinded many that they believe they are the owner of their bodies and can do to it what they like. That is a very big lie. God owns your body and it is His temple (1 Cor. 3:16). Once ignorance succeeds in moving you to commit fornication and adultery, God Himself, not even other things, will destroy you. Why? It is because you defile His temple which is your body. This is the truth you must know. Everything sweet is always dangerous to our body and health. Not all that is glitters is gold. If you can't control your body anymore, it will be better to marry instead of bringing God's judgment upon your life. If you are already married and you are still committing adultery, you are only exposing your life to serious danger and destruction. God who created human in the beginning created them male and female (Gen. 1:27) and not male and females or males and female. This means God created a man to be committed to a woman and not women; likewise, He created a woman to be committed to a man and not men. It is a tragedy that teenagers and youths are involving in such destructive practice. You are only harming yourself and not others. You may be enjoying it now, but the truth is that you are actually sowing to your future and may affect your eternity if you don't stop the act. When you lust after a woman or man or men or women, you

have already committed fornication or adultery with him or her or them (Matt. 5:28). When you watch pornography, strip yourself naked for people to see, or love people that are doing such things, you are already committing fornication and adultery. This is a great weapon in the hands of ignorance to destroy people. Be aware and be vigilant.

19.   Hatred: Hatred is a weapon in the hands of ignorance. It is understood that when you hate your brethren or fellow human being, you are not only harming yourself but also transgressing against God's commandment for this dispensation of grace. God has perfected everything that what you need to survive is present in other people around you or far from you. But the mystery behind it is that you don't know the particular person because you are limited by what you see. Now, imagine you hate the person who has been destined to move your life forward. The hatred in you will definitely allow you to always avoid the person. Ignorance will so much do it that it will create a great distance between you and your helpers so that you won't come into terms (agreement), talk less of him or her helping. You can even go to the extent of fighting with the person. This is the reason why God commanded us to love our neighbors. The person you trust to love may not be the person who will save you from destruction and can even be the one to lead you into destruction. The best is to love all. There is no excuse for hatred. All excuses for hating your brethren are only a fuel to increase the fire of judgment upon you. Owe no man anything but to

love another. You don't have everything you need to prosper in life. Your fulfillment in life depends on other people who have been assigned to you. You can't achieve that greatness without people helping you. God will not come down to help you, but He will use the fellow brethren whom you love or hate. This is what ignorance has used to destroy many. Loving your brethren is not optional but a commandment. When you continue to hate people, you are only breeding yourself on the platform of failure and destruction.

20. Gluttony: Gluttony signifies ignorance at work. It is very easy to poison a glutton. Gluttons don't hesitate to eat anything edible and can also eat poison. Gluttons are always eating to their destruction. They are easy to use as a scapegoat. They are scapegrace. Gluttons don't invest because they lavish everything they have to satisfy their stomach. Nobody wants to work with a glutton. A glutton will always bring losses to one's accounts. People always run away from them. The gluttons should be aware of destruction because there won't be anyone to tell them when they are about to enter to destruction since everybody would flee from them.

21. Abusive words: Abusive words are a sign of ignorance. Our words carry power, and our tongue is full of deadly poison (James 3:8). Most words spoken by us don't lie fallow but usually accomplish its mission. When it goes out of your mouth, it goes straight to accomplish its mission, and when it can't accomplish the mission, it returns back to you. Likewise, when you curse or abuse someone, if it fails to be established on the person addressed,

it returns back to you. Every words coming out of your mouth are spirits, and they don't die but rather are stored up or sown for reaping. If you are ignorant of this, you are doing nothing but planning your days of destruction. Ignorance do a great job by blinding people from being aware of this so that it will be much easy to destroy them.

22. Curse: Curses are used to destroy destiny. Curse makes one's life miserable. Curses can be generational. That is, it can be acquired from family. It can be issued against one by God, people, devil, and his agent. Curse from God is always on wicked people and disobedient who fail to repent. Wait a minute and examine yourself whether you are a wicked man or woman or boy or girl or young man or lady? Then, know definitely that this curse is upon you unless you repent. The truth is that when God curses you, or He is the one behind your problem because of your evil deeds, no power can deliver you out from His hand because all powers belong to Him. I advise you to repent because it is a very dangerous thing to fall into hands of God (Heb. 10:31). If man or woman or devil curses you, you can still run to your Creator to save you, but no one can save you if God curses you. You should also know that when you are cursed or blessed, it will affect your seeds (Heb. 7:9). Ignorance can move you to offend people so that they curse you. And sometimes ignorance move people to curse without a cause. But because a curse without a cause cannot stand (Prov. 26:2), the curse returns back to the sender. You must avoid anything that can bring curses upon your life.

23. Dirtiness: A dirty person is close to destruction because dirtiness embraces destruction. Dirtiness causes unpleasant smells that are harmful to our health. Dirtiness also produces bacteria and parasites that can kill people. Dirtiness exposes one's life to destruction. Ignorance causes dirtiness. A dirty person is always attacked by different disease and sickness. A dirty environment causes parasites, bacteria, and odors that kill untimely. A dirty environment and houses or rooms expose you to dangers. A dirty life attracts sicknesses, disfavor, hatred, etcetera. You need knowledge to get rid of this. You must destroy this weapon of ignorance if you want to live a peaceful and a clean life. Dirtiness is dangerous to your life, so avoid it.

24. Wastage: Wastage is also a weapon of destruction (ignorance). Wasters waste all things including grace to survive. God hates wastage that He told the men to gather the remaining bread and fish left after He fed five thousand people (John 6:12). God don't entrust resources and precious things into the hands of a waster. Some even have all that it takes to make them great, but ignorance controls them and make them to waste all the resources they have. It knows that once it succeeds in wasting those resources given to them, it will be easy to destroy them. A waster is not far from destruction. Wasters are wastes themselves. They don't care about other people and things entrusted or given to them.

25. Jealousy: When you are bitter about other's life or things, you should be aware of ignorance dragging you to a place of destruction. Jealousy moves one to committing murder and other dangerous act.

Jealousy creates a great bitterness and hatred which put one in a confusion and mind disorderliness. Negative jealousy makes you a wicked person and a destroyer. Don't be confused because I said negative jealousy. Jealousy can be expressed in negative and positive ways. Jealousy in a positive or good ways means guiding particular things or watching over them because of love and passion you have for those things. A very good example is when you guide your children and wife jealousy from evil because of the love you have for them. But negative jealousy means bitter reaction concerning other possessions. Avoid jealousy to avoid ignorance.

CHAPTER FIVE

KNOWLEDGE

Having explained the levels, truths, and weapons of ignorance, let us look more into knowledge, truths about it, and ways to get it.

Knowledge is from the word *know*. And to know, you have to deal with information. What you know determines the kind of life you will live. When you know something, the things you know or information you get is the knowledge. That is, knowledge comes as information, and it is knowledge because it is needed to be known.

The first truth you must know about knowledge is that it is from God. That is, the source of knowledge is God. Any other knowledge apart from this is counterfeit knowledge.

As I have said earlier, knowledge is the only cure for ignorance. Without knowledge, mankind will perish.

Knowledge is what opens one's eyes to see the right things. It is what makes you know what is good and bad. We may have been doing wrong things, but as soon as we get the right knowledge that we need, light is shed on the darkness and will make us realize our mistakes.

No one can claim to be hundred percent full of knowledge that he or she does not need any more knowledge. Getting knowledge is a process that continues till we die. This means, we keep seeking knowledge so as to survive the terror created by ignorance every day.

The greatest thing to do when it comes to the aspect of knowledge is to dwell with it (knowledge) at all time so that it can feed us daily with what is needed to be known. I am actually saying you are supposed to work with knowledge at all time to avoid ignorance in your life. We need to commune with knowledge daily and every hour so that it can save us from the terror of ignorance.

Ignorance is always there, seeking who to devour because it works with the devil to fulfill the devil's agendas for mankind. The tragedy is that anytime it goes out with the mission to devour people, it always finds many who lacks knowledge (Hosea 4:6).

Knowledge has levels. But your level in knowledge depends on your relationship with it. That is, your distance to it depends on the knowledge you will have. When you make knowledge your friend, what you won't know is only what you don't need to know. As ignorance is a spirit, so knowledge is also a spirit (Isa. 11:2).

Knowledge works with wisdom and understanding. When knowledge is without wisdom and understanding, it becomes mystery. If you want to be a friend of knowledge, you must be wise enough to accept it and understand it. This means, knowledge is not effective without wisdom and understanding.

When you seek knowledge without wisdom and understanding, it may kill you. That is the reason why there is a general saying that too much knowledge kills. Wisdom and understanding will let you know the right level or parts of knowledge you need and amount or measure you are capable of withstanding. But when you claim to accept knowledge and reject wisdom and understanding, you have only accepted what will kill you. What I am saying is that there is a kind of knowledge you need (knowledge appears in different forms or ways) and the level you must get to. It is just like a university, where we can find different faculties, departments, and courses.

The best way to attain a good level of knowledge is to thirst for more every day. You can't be a champion in the school of knowledge with just few days or years of enrollment.

Chapter Six

TRUTHS ABOUT KNOWLEDGE

With the brief introduction of knowledge, let us look at about eighty-seven truths to know about knowledge.

1. It appears in different forms: Knowledge exists in different forms at different situations and cases. That is why we can say we have different kinds of knowledge. But it is still one spirit. Our area of needs determine the kinds or forms of knowledge we will get. Because of its different forms of existence, we can categorize knowledge as educational knowledge, moral knowledge, spiritual knowledge, physical knowledge, and so on. Remember that I have told you earlier when I was discussing the truths about ignorance that it can disguise itself as knowledge. So, you should not believe all knowledge that comes your way, but test it. Knowledge appears in many ways but cannot appear to produce death. The knowledge that you know that produces death is actually ignorance. The best example for this is when you study to destroy yourself or keep studying irrelevant things; in this case, you are actually toiling with ignorance and not the true knowledge. Not all studying involve the true knowledge. Not in all cases you go to school to get knowledge. It is possible to spend most of one's life in school in acquiring ignorance

that will kill you. Studying hard to acquire ignorance (counterfeit knowledge) makes you a fool. So if you are a professor based on ignorance acquired, you become a foolish professor. I'm not against professors. Knowledge has some distinct character that makes it to be true knowledge and not a counterfeit. Any person who claims to have knowledge and still have some of the characters ascribed to ignorance is actually ignorant and not knowledgeable.

2. It is big: Knowledge is so big that it has many levels or rooms that are yet to be occupied. No one can get to the end of knowledge, no matter how fast you are. Studying everyday and minute will not guarantee that you get to its end. You only see the end of knowledge when you die. It is when you die that you won't need it anymore. Knowledge has never complained of having too many friends and candidates but is still looking for more. It is so big that it can fill and satisfy as many who seek it. When you think you have arrived at its destination, it is at that point you have just started the journey of knowledge. However, you are greater than the person who hasn't got to your level.

3. It teaches: Knowledge will teach you to know what you are supposed to know. It works with understanding. Understanding should follow when knowledge appears. Knowledge without understanding is still ignorance. Knowledge is the information needed, and understanding is the interpretation of the knowledge. Don't get confused; wisdom, knowledge, and understanding work together as one because you can't apply knowledge without understanding it. Is it not

what you know that you believe? Dictionary meaning also says understanding is the knowledge of something. Let me give you an example of what this means: knowledge will make a poor man to know that he's really poor; if the poor man accepts the knowledge, understanding will then explain and make him believe the knowledge. Since he has believed and intends to be free from poverty, knowledge then opens his eyes to see the tools and substance needed for him to be rich. Understanding will make him to know the relevant and how important the tools and substances are. Then, wisdom will give him the correct application of the knowledge he has gotten. When a person is wise, you say he or she has knowledge. So also is when someone is knowledgeable, you will say he or she has wisdom or understanding. Wisdom, knowledge, and understanding work together as one. Knowledge does not stop at letting you know the right thing but teaches you with understanding.

4. It is power: Knowledge is power. Knowledgeable person is much better than a mighty illiterate. It is better than weapons of war (Eccles. 9:18). With knowledge, you can get the kind of powers you need. You can also defeat any battle with knowledge. When you become a best friend of knowledge, you will be more powerful compared to an ignorant person. Knowledge rules powers. That is, it is a genuine power and also rules over ordinary powers. It is very difficult to defeat a knowledgeable person.

5. It is an enemy of ignorance: Ignorance and knowledge have never been in oneness. You can't

be a friend of knowledge and at the same time, friend of ignorance. You have to choose one. It is either you are growing in knowledge (partial ignorant), or you are completely ignorant. They never agreed, talk less of working with each other. Another reason why they can never be in good terms is that they have different agendas. The agenda of ignorance is to destroy because it works with the devil, while the agenda of knowledge is to give life and it works with God and is from Him. They are opposite.

6.   It is the only weapon to kill ignorance: From ancient time till date, knowledge still remains the only weapon to kill ignorance. No weapon has been approved or will be approved against ignorance. Trying to kill ignorance with an ignorant is like breeding a small snake to make it bigger and wider than before. When you use an ignorant against ignorance, you are only preparing a hard judgment of ignorance against yourself.

7.   It destroys ignorance: Knowledge is the only weapon to destroy ignorance. If you want to be free from ignorance, you need to seek knowledge and be its friend. The level of your ignorance will determine the level of knowledge you will need, in other words, to be free from ignorance. Knowledge is a fear and terror to ignorance. Ignorance always avoids knowledge. It (ignorance) knows that knowledge will not only send it (ignorance) out of its territory but also destroy its territory so that it has no place again.

8.   It makes ignorance's territory to be desolate: As I was saying, knowledge is a great barrier and terror to ignorance. Knowledge makes ignorance's

territory or place to be completely empty or desolate. Where knowledge dominates or inhabits, it will be very difficult to locate ignorance. Likewise, whenever knowledge is allowed to take over maybe a territory, it will completely eradicate ignorance. If you want to completely empty the works of ignorance in your life, you need to allow knowledge to rule your life. You need to be careful so that you won't devout your time in acquiring ignorance.

9. It is expensive and can be easily obtained: Knowledge is expensive, and at the same time, it is cheap. Whether it is cheap or expensive depends on you. Most of the time, knowledge comes cheaply to us at early stage of life, but when we refuse it at the time it came, it will become very expensive later and when needed. Also, when knowledge appears to be cheap, it comes along with grace so that we can receive it with ease. But when we refuse it, as a result of ignorance, it becomes more expensive without grace to even accept it again. It is ignorance that makes you feel knowledge is too expensive. The knowledge you think is expensive now will surely be a great asset to you later so that you earn the square portion of what you have sacrificed for it. In fact, knowledge obtained through sacrifice yields great reward than the one obtained in a cheap way. You don't need to complain about the price to pay for knowledge. The only thing you need to do is to be sure it is a genuine knowledge and make sure it is the actual knowledge you need. I said "actual knowledge you need" because we have different levels and aspects in knowledge as I have told you earlier. There are

ones you need and ones you don't need, although no knowledge is lost. It is just like a student who wants to study mechanical engineering course doesn't need to spend time reading biology.

10. It does not act without permission: Knowledge will only rule your life if you permit it. It acts on your permission. It helps you when you seek it. It is ignorance that appears without invitation. Knowledge will always wait for permission before taking over. People only value what they seek, long, and suffer for. When you seek knowledge, you will value it than a person who got it on a platter of gold. You will always find knowledge in the position you put it in your life. This means, if you put it outside your affairs, you can never by any means find it inside.

11. It says the truth: There is no deceit or lie in knowledge. If you have ever seen knowledge that entails lies or deceits, then you need to question it whether it is truly knowledge or ignorance. Knowledge always says the truth. Anyone who claims to be knowledgeable and is a liar is ignorant. This is how a knowledgeable person is differentiated from a person who is ignorant. Knowledge will always tell you that a lying tongue will surely ends in destruction. No matter who you are and what your position, dignitary, level of anointing, or kind of calling is, if you are a liar, whether white lies or red lies, you are ignorant and signing to end your life in destruction.

12. It does not steal: Knowledge is not enticed by others' properties. It is impossible to see knowledge stealing. One of the characteristics of knowledge is contentment. If you claim to be knowledgeable,

stealing should not be ascribed to you. You should not desire or be carried away with other's properties, talk less of stealing. Any person found stealing is ignorant. Stealing is as a result of ignorance.

13. It gives life: Knowledge is to produce life wherever it dominates. When you know it and apply it, it will surely give you life. The Bible says in Hosea 4:6 that the people of God perish for lack of knowledge. What makes them to perish was lack of knowledge and not its presence. That tells us that its presence will surely give them life (Prov. 11:9). It is just like a man who committed suicide. He did so because he was ignorant that life will still exist after killing himself, the world will not end because of his death, his family will only mourn for few days, his wife and children will not stop living because he's gone, and the problem he's facing will surely end. If he had gotten these knowledge when he was about to end himself, the knowledge would have given him life. Eventually, because he lacks knowledge, he killed himself. Ignorance is a bad guy. If you want to live long, you need to get knowledge and grow in it every day.

14. It is honest: Knowledge is known for honesty. A dishonest person is ignorant. Knowledge is always faithful in little and has no pretentions. Honesty is a good character that makes you qualify for opportunities. In fact, a dishonest person can't work with God. Take time to examine yourself whether you are honest or not? If you are not, it shows you are ignorant and need knowledge to be free. It is when you have the knowledge of honesty

and reward behind honesty, it is then you will always want to be honest in everything you do.

15. It is straight forward or plain. Knowledge is not cunning. Knowledge is always plain. A cunning person is never known by knowledge neither should he or she claims to have it. Cunning behavior is a dangerous character that must not be found in a person's life. What made Esau to lose his birthright was because of his cunning character. God said he hate Esau, not because He wants the covenant He made with Abraham to be established in Jacob, but because Esau was a cunning man. A cunning person is crafty and a liar. And you know the Bible mentioned those things that God hates in which this thing was found (Prov. 6:16). The Bible described Esau as a cunning man and Jacob as a plain man even as they were growing up (Gen. 25:27). Esau taught he will use his cunning wisdom to get food without submitting his birthright, not knowing that Jacob also had a different plan for him because Jacob himself was a supplanter. The cunning character of Esau made him lose his birthright. When you think you are smart to cheat someone, know that you are digging a hole for yourself. Craftiness or cunning character will always take something tangible from you.

16. It is light: It is light that shines to eradicate darkness. No one can work in a thick darkness until light appears. Darkness is an hour for wickedness. Wickedness is not done during the day because all the evil will be revealed for judgment. Darkness is the hour when different kinds of wicked agenda are carried out. But when

light comes, every wicked deeds will be revealed and people can freely work without stumbling. That is why God promised to be a light unto His people so that they won't stumble (Ps. 119:105, Isa. 60:19, Mic. 7:8, Matt. 5:15, Acts 26:23). When knowledge comes, it sheds light to the darkness so that the deeds in the dark hour may be revealed and its victim may live instead of being destroyed. A person without knowledge is in total darkness and such needs light to put away the darkness that has dominated his or her life.

17. It makes you a friend of God: An ignorant person can never be a friend of God because he won't comprehend the things of God, talk less of working right to please Him. God wants His people to seek and get knowledge. In fact, when the Holy Spirit of God comes upon one to exhibit God's power, he also gives other things in which knowledge is parts (Isa. 11:2). It will now depend whether the person is willing to use the knowledge or not. God won't force you because He already says His Spirit will not strife with men (Gen. 6:3). The book of Deuteronomy 30:19 says ". . . . I have set before you life and death, blessing and cursing: therefore choose life." This means, life has been made available for us, likewise death is also around but you are advised to choose life. If you want to be a friend of God, you need to always long for and make use of knowledge. The truth is that God teaches and we can say He is a Teacher (Exod. 4:12, Ps. 18:34, Ps. 25:4, Ps. 32:8, Matt. 22:16, 1 Cor. 2:13). This means that for you to be His friend, you must always listen to Him and learn so that you can get knowledge.

18. It produces good character: You can always differentiate a knowledgeable person from an ignorant person in terms of character. Ignorance is behind bad character, while knowledge produces good character. It will help you and guide you from bad characters. What I am saying is that one of the characteristics or way to know a good person is a good character.

19. It makes you to overcome challenges: Challenges are overcome with the help of knowledge. Ignorance makes a challenge a danger so that one is killed. Knowledge will let you know that there is no victory without a challenge, challenges are force or resistance to a success or breakthrough and must be overcome, life is entangled with various challenges, what makes you a champion is as the result of the challenges you've faced in the past, gold is never found on the earth but beneath or inside the earth, failure is not the end of life but opportunity to get something better and uncommon, the general and champion are ones who have faced various challenges and overcame them, challenges is a key or steps to one's breakthroughs, and so on. But ignorance will always hide all these from you. If you want to overcome the challenges you are facing now or the ones you will face later, you need to get knowledge.

20. It cures disease: A diseased person needs drug or something to cure his or her diseases. What knowledge does is to first let you know the truth that you are diseased, tells you the type and the cause, the solution, the right people to meet, and the kind of drugs to take or things to do. It will

always take a knowledgeable person to accept a fault and seek for solutions. But an ignorant person will not even accept the truth that he is diseased, and if he eventually accepts that, he will end up in meeting the wrong people and taking the wrong drugs. It is knowledge that provides solution or cure to all kinds of diseases you can mention. Drugs and other means of curing disease are made by knowledge.

21.   It guides you from evil: The Bible passage we read as our reference in the beginning of the discussion tells us that people of God perish because of lack of knowledge (Hosea 4:6). And the Bible also mentions good and evil that is set before us (Deut. 30:19). Knowledge lets you run and depart from evil. Ignorant people are easily ensnared by evils.

22.   It elevates you to the top: Knowledge makes you the best in the area you applied it. For example, if you want to be the best (be at the top) in your academics, you need to move closer and go deep into knowledge. Also, if you want to be the best or get to the highest level, you need to get to an unusual part of knowledge. Knowledge is the first prerequisite to being a general or the best. The level you found yourself now is as a result of knowledge you got. Your level of knowledge determines your level in life. Are you satisfied with your position in your education, career, or any place you are now? Did you want to go higher or to the top? If yes, then you need to seek knowledge the more. What makes an eagle a habitant of mountain and rider of the sky without fair of the storm is as a result of the knowledge God created it with. This has differentiated it from other birds you may talk about.

23. It makes one a celebrity: Knowledge makes you to be famous. That is to be well known in terms of excellence. However, ignorance also makes you famous but in terms of failure. It is left for you to choose the kind you want. Knowledge will make you to be celebrated. The level of celebration also depends on the level of knowledge. Just like in the case of students where the best student will be celebrated, likewise the second and the third. But the way each will be celebrated differs because of the level of knowledge and achievements.

24. It makes one a general: When you seek and go very deep into knowledge, then, you will be able to do extraordinary things on earth that will make you to become a general. To be a general is not what can be obtained with ignorance. Knowledge must be sought in the specialized area of field. The general I mean is to be a high-ranking person in the world either when living or after death. I also mean to impact life in a good way, to be a good celebrity, and to be an uncommon person in terms of good works. For example, if you want to be a general maybe in the area of discovery, then you will need knowledge to approach a particular problem or challenge so as to create a solution by discovering an unusual thing or method or way in which the problems and challenges faced by people will be solved. Of all the generals that have ever existed, no one had ever made use of ignorance to succeed, because it is a killer of destiny.

25. It teaches mystery: Most of the time, knowledge comes in mystery and teaches in mystery. That is why understanding is needed. But the good thing is that so far you accept knowledge and make it

your friend, understanding and wisdom will definitely follow you. When you reject wisdom and understanding, you can never succeed in the school of knowledge. The three work together. That is wisdom, knowledge, and understanding will make you a complete person. It also helps in spiritual matters. This is the reason why it seems as if knowledge kills, because people only got it without wisdom and understanding. You need wisdom and understanding to rightly apply the knowledge you have obtained, or else it will kill you. Knowledge has always been a mystery to those who do not use it. It doesn't appear simple to them and is not easily understood.

26. It does not give room for laziness:—any person who wants to work successfully with knowledge must first deal with his or her laziness. Laziness can never be found in the dictionary of knowledge because it itself is obtained by hardworking. Anytime a lazy person come across knowledge or opportune to get knowledge, he will miss the opportunity because his laziness will make him incapable to work with knowledge. Lazy people are ignorant. Hardworking people are always found in the school of Knowledge. A lazy person is a great failure in the school of Knowledge.

27. It encourages: Knowledge is always there to encourage us especially in times of trouble and also in any situations. Whenever problems arise, knowledge will tell you there is a way out and will also provide you with the solution if you allow it. People of knowledge don't easily give up; they are not imprisoned or permanently captured by their problems. They always encourage others with

profitable words and not useless one. If you claim to be knowledgeable and you give up easily or you are not always encouraged in a situation, you need to check yourself. It might be that you have not allowed or sought knowledge in the situation or you refuse it to help you.

28.   It makes one to be strong: Knowledgeable people are strong, and they cannot be easily pulled down. Making knowledge your friend is like hiding in a rock. To build yourself on the platform of knowledge is like building your house on a rock. People with knowledge are not easily defeated, and some cannot be defeated at all because of their level and relationship with knowledge. If you seek knowledge in your education, career, finances, marital life, and other areas of life, you will be strong in those areas in which you have allowed it.

29.   It produces neatness: One of the products of knowledge is neatness. Dirtiness is never found in knowledge. Dirty people who claim to be knowledgeable are still ignorant because dirtiness attracts death. The best way to know a knowledgeable person is in term of neatness. However, you may be neat and still be ignorant. This is because you have only made use of the knowledge or allowed it in your area of cleanliness and maybe refusing it in other areas. Any place, environment, country, home where knowledge dominates, neatness has always been their beauty.

30.   It makes one wise: As I said earlier, wisdom, knowledge, and understanding work together to give perfection. When you seek knowledge and make it your friend, it will also introduce you to wisdom which is its partner. A word of knowledge

makes one to be wise. When you reject the words of knowledge, you become a fool.

31. It is obtained by searching: Knowledge is mostly obtained by those who seek or search for it. Knowledge obtained without seeking will have no value in the sight of the person who got it and may not impact the life. Knowledge is not hard to find when we seek it with all of our heart. It is a spirit. The reason why we find it difficult to get knowledge when we seek it is because we don't search in the right way when seeking it and also we only search for it with our lips.

32. It is obtained by longsuffering and perseverance: Those who long for knowledge are always found by it. Sometimes when you seek knowledge for a particular thing, it may not appear immediately. It will require patience and continuous action to get it. To get knowledge sometimes requires endurance depending on the deepness of the knowledge you are looking for. Let me explain with this simple analogy: let's assume knowledge is like the earth. You can dig inside for many reasons. Now, every good thing you can see or touch is presently on and inside this earth. But where you will find those things depends on their values. That is, you can't find gold and crude oil on the surface of the earth, but you need to dig very deep into earth to see all these things. And no one knows the exact square kilometers in which these things are located. You will need patience to continue digging until you find them. Any gold found on the top surface of the earth may be a perverse one. Likewise is knowledge. Any knowledge obtained cheaply has low values compared to ones obtained

by seeking and longsuffering, although every knowledge is useful.

33.   It is obtained by loving: Most knowledge is obtained from people you know and those you did not know. Love is the only commandment given by God in the New Testament (John 15:17). There are things you have and others don't have; likewise, there are things others have that you don't have. The mystery behind this is that both what they and you have are things needed for all to survive and there can't be any way to share on these things without loving each other. Your neighbor has the knowledge you did not have. When you hate him or her, you will remain a victim of ignorance and life may not be guaranteed. You can't acquire knowledge from someone or things you hate. In fact, if you want to get knowledge or things from God and desire to enter His peace and rest, you need to love Him with all your heart by putting Him first in all aspects of your life (Mark 12:30). Another truth is that you will only get knowledge when you love it. Anyone who hates knowledge is traveling at a very high speed to the land of destruction.

34.   It is obtained by learning: As I have said earlier, it is a common saying that readers are leaders, but I proved it wrong and rather say, learners are leaders. What makes you a leader or a very good leader is the result of knowledge you have obtained. This knowledge is obtained from what you learned either through reading or what you listen to or experience. Getting knowledge goes beyond reading books but learning from what you are reading and putting them into practice. When

you read for fun, you are not getting knowledge. Likewise, when you read bad books, you are only acquiring ignorance that will destroy you. What I'm telling you is that what makes reading effective is learning, and then you will acquire knowledge through it. A good learner is a knowledgeable person. In the Bible, David says blessed be the Lord who teaches my hands to war (2 Sam. 22:35, Ps. 18:34, Ps. 144:1). That is, what he learned gave him good knowledge about warfare. When you are learning to repair, to build and so on, you will get enough knowledge of those things learned. The summary of what I am saying is that learning is a good way of acquiring knowledge. Knowledge is a friend to a learner.

35. It is obtained by listening: A good listener is a wise and knowledgeable person. The Bible tells us to be swift to hear and slow to speak (James: 1:19). Listening here means to pay attention to words so as to learn from it and not busy bodying and gossiping. You don't need to speak at all times but need to hear at all times. When God created you, He gave you two eyes so that you can see clearly at all times. He gave you nose or nostrils so that you can have a sharp smell sensitivity, He gave you two ears so that you can hear every word clearly, but he gave you one mouth so that you speak when necessary and not all time. Knowledge mostly comes as words which must be listened to in order to get its message. Knowledge is a friend to a listener.

36. It is obtained by reading: Knowledge is also obtained from reading. It is not obtained when you read for fun, but it is obtained when you

read to learn and acquire knowledge. There is knowledge that you will only get through no other way but reading. Like what you are reading now, you cannot see me nor do I, but I'm passing this knowledge to you through a book. A lazy person cannot get this knowledge I am passing across to the world. Not all knowledge will be spoken to you. There are some that will be written for you to read. When you read a book, don't just read to catch fun but read to learn from it. That is why you must be careful of the type of books you read because ignorance can also be acquired from books. Knowledge is a friend to a reader.

37. It is a key: Knowledge is a key to many doors and especially to success. A key is what gives you access to something. It is also what you can use to control something. We can say that knowledge is a key to any good thing in life, while ignorance is also a key to bad things and death. If you want to be great in life, to succeed, to get rid of something, to get solutions to a problem, to be free, access to a position and level, access to a place, and so on, you need a key which is knowledge. It is the only key to get hidden things, riches, substance, etcetera. Knowledge is an essential key to life.

38. It makes you an extraordinary person: As I said earlier, it makes you a general. It also makes you an extraordinary person. That is, you are no more like an ordinary person. You now have honor that differentiates you from others. You carry something special. You don't behave like an ordinary person, especially like a person without purpose and vision, and you are no more a common person but an extraordinary one.

Ordinary people are people without purpose or vision or people who don't fulfill destiny but rather live their life for fun and excitements.

39. It makes you do extraordinary things: I have told you that knowledge is a key. When you get knowledge, you already have a key to exploit, and it is left for you to use it. Knowledge is a key or secret behind great exploits. When God wants to use people for His work, He gave them knowledge as part of gifts (Isa. 11:2). If you want to perform exploits in life, you must have its key which is knowledge. And don't just have but use it.

40. It makes one to be always victorious: I have told you before that you can't defeat a knowledgeable person, or he or she is not easily defeated. They may fall but will always rise again. They may encounter serious or terrible problems but will be victorious at last. Knowledge will always provide solutions to problems; it is a solution provider. One must be sensitive to it because it can speak through any person you may not expect. It speaks to you through what you read and can even speak directly to you. Yes, knowledge speaks.

41. It makes peace: Knowledge is not found to create troubles or cause violence but rather make peace. Whenever a trouble or violence occurs, it takes any other thing than knowledge to settle it and to allow peace. A knowledgeable person is also a peacemaker because he or she will know that trouble or violence will lead to destruction and death. Ignorance causes violence and trouble. Until one has the knowledge and understanding of what peace entails, it will be impossible to be a peacemaker. Not all gentleness is peace. A gentle

person can cause violence even with his or her gentleness. It is mostly said that a gentle person is a dangerous person because they can do you more harm than an outspoken person. Outspoken people will let you know when they are angry so that they can settle everything immediately without keeping malice. I'm not saying it is bad to be gentle. What I am saying is that it is one thing to be gentle and another thing to be a peacemaker or to be gentle in spirit. True sons of God are expected to make peace at all times (Matt. 5:9). An outspoken person can likewise be a peacemaker. It may be that he or she did not like to be silent when something is going wrong but prefer to talk for peace to reign. It is possible for a gentle person to be calm until everything gets spoiled. The best is to be gentle and likewise be a peacemaker.

42. It gives long-life: Anyone who wants to live long needs knowledge. Knowledge is needed to know what is good and bad for your health, the right and wrong places to go, the best time to do things, the right food to eat, the right drinks to drink, the right friend to have, the right job to do, the best time to act, what to abstain from or avoid, what to go for, how to manage your health, how to treat yourself, and how to recognize and flee from danger. When all these things are not known or fully understood, it shortens one's life.

43. It increases your achievement: The deeper you are in knowledge, the more your achievements will be. No one has ever achieved anything good or bad without knowledge or ignorance. Knowledge and ignorance determine the kind of achievements you will have. Also, the level of your knowledge

determines the achievement you will have. When you study for the level of a doctor, then you will become a doctor. Likewise, when you study for the level of a professor, you will become one. You can't go far from the level of your knowledge.

44.   It makes one to understand what is right and wrong: It is behind moral. It is knowledge that makes us to differentiate between what is right and wrong, evil and good. It is difficult for an ignorant person to truly and thoroughly differentiate right from wrong. Most of the time wrong will be misinterpreted as right. This is caused by ignorance. It will be a big tragedy for an ignorant person to be made a judge or leader because he will always call what is wrong right. In order words, knowledge helps to give true justice.

45.   It gives joy: Knowledge always brings great happiness to the people who have it. It gives them victory, promotion, peace, and honor and makes them great and unique. Ignorance will always sadden its victim because it has nothing good to offer. Even in times of troubles, knowledgeable people are always in peace and they have joy in their heart because they know that they will surely win.

46.   It builds: Building entails joining two or parts together to form a powerful structure. To build is also an act of developing things into big structure. Building may be physical structure, intellectual, spiritual, moral, and other invisible things. In one word, building is achieved by thinking and creativeness. Right thinking and creativeness are made possible by the help of knowledge. With the help of knowledge, powerful structures have been built and more of it is still expected to be built.

47.   It kills illiteracy: Knowledge is an effective poison to illiteracy. Illiteracy can't survive if it drinks the beverages of knowledge. Knowledge has always been a good weapon to eradicate illiteracy. The best time to apply a pesticide is when the pests are not fully grown or when they have not taken full ground in one's life. If it is applied after many things have been destroyed, things lost may never be recovered.

48.   It abides with the wise: A major characteristic of the wise is that they are knowledgeable. Wisdom is a container in which knowledge dwells. It is a fluid that allows knowledge to flow freely. Understanding is that which reveals and make knowledge simple. When you see a wise man, you will be sure to acquire knowledge from him. Words of knowledge will only proceed out of the mouth of the wise. It is only the wise that have access to knowledge. In other words, the license to knowledge is wisdom.

49.   It changes people's outlook and physical nature: Knowledge does not only change your mind, sense, moral, attitude, and so on, but also changes your outlook. It is possible to recognize people of knowledge by their physical appearance: they are not proud, don't have a proud look, are not easily provoked, think before they open their mouth, are not violent, are gentle both outside and inside, dress corporately, have a sense of color and pattern combination in dressing, work with authority and not with fear, are fast to hear and slow to speak, show kindness, look natural to appreciate how God created them, are proud of who they are, dress moderately, don't lie, show respect to whom

respect is due to, are always willing to be a help to people, are humble, and so on. Anyone who claims to have knowledge without any sign in his or her physical life is a liar.

50.   It enhances people's thinking: Knowledge will always give you questions to answer in order to build you and enhance your thinking. Anytime you need a solution to a problem, you will need to think before you get the solution. What you eventually get through your thinking will then become an experience and solution that can never be forgotten. This will also make it easy to get solutions to other related problems. That is the reason why knowledgeable people don't have time for nonsense but spend time to settle and refresh their thinking so as to get and develop their knowledge.

51.   It accelerates people's thinking speed: Knowledgeable people think faster. Once they encounter a problem, their senses quickly search for solution inside knowledge. That is why it is always good to have a knowledgeable person beside when facing troubles because he will always provide solution without wasting time. Another reason knowledge enhances fast thinking is that all solutions are present in it; the only thing needed is to look for a solution. A person who has made knowledge his partner will easily work in to get what he wants without wasting time.

52.   It is deep and has levels: As I have told you earlier, knowledge is very deep, and we are supposed to keep going into it every day. In fact, you can't get to its end till you die. It is ignorant people who claim to have known all about knowledge. The faster you move does not make you get

closer to its end but will only change your level. Knowledge is also like a very big mansion with a lot of departments and rooms. You only need to go directly to where you fit. An attempt to log in into other place that does not fit you may kill you. This is caused by ignorance. Ignorance will always allow one to pursue the kind of knowledge (department or section) that is not needed. Every level you get to in your journey in knowledge contributes to your life. Also you must always desire to move to higher level every time because all levels have their own useful moment and expiry date.

53. It gives riches: Anyone who wants to be rich needs knowledge. It is knowledge that tells you what to do and how to do in order to get rich. The level of your knowledge determines your level of riches. An attempt to be richer than one's level is a fraudulent act. Those riches will be obtained by fraudulent act. The reason why you are still poor is that you lack knowledge or lack a particular knowledge needed or have not obtained the right section of knowledge needed. When I mean riches, I'm referring to riches not only in financial aspect but also in all areas of life because it is possible to be very rich financially and materially but poor in idea, health, intellectual, etcetera. In fact, ignorance mostly captures the rich (financially and materially) easily. A true riche is not having all the material things including money on earth but having prosperity in all things without lacking the peace of God (3 John 1:2).

54. It produces humility: Humility and humble life are a product of knowledge. People who profess to be knowledgeable and are proud or not humble

are ignorant. Knowledge has not taken hold of their life, or they have only given knowledge a few places in their life. That is, there is still ignorance roaming about their life. Small or little ignorance is enough to destroy one. Ignorance only needs a small chance to destroy all what have been acquired by knowledge. It is an empty container that makes louder noise or sound when hit, but a filled one will never produce sound. Likewise, knowledgeable people live a humble life and not a proud or violent life to show they are knowledgeable. People of knowledge don't seek vain glory.

55. It makes you the best: It is knowledge that makes one to excel beyond colleagues and counterparts. As I have said earlier, it will make you to do extraordinary things that will differentiate you from others. Being the best is not an easy task because you have to go beyond ordinary by doing what others don't do. If others are in a particular level of knowledge, then you need to upgrade yourself to a higher level if truly you are ready to be the best. It is the knowledge you pursue and the one gained that makes you to excel among your colleagues. Knowledge goes before excellence.

56. It is always available: You are the one who will decide when you want to acquire knowledge. It is always available and ready to help. When you seek knowledge so late, you will eventually find it, but you may not recover all that has been lost. The problem that most people are facing, especially in the issue of knowledge, is procrastination. We try to set time for ourselves and by so doing postponing the time to seek knowledge. It is

good to seek knowledge earlier and not at the late hour. You will always find knowledge whenever you think it is the best time for you to acquire it. However, it may not work for you at that time because of the late hour you seek it. Always set your priority right.

57. It is special, that is, uncommon: Knowledge is not a common thing, especially the deep areas of knowledge. That makes it expensive. Anyone who seeks knowledge is always uncommon and special because knowledge itself is special and not common. The part of knowledge you find common or you think is common is only the scrape parts of it which can be obtained by anyone. Knowledge is being bought with money, time, sacrifice, and other valuable things because it is very great. Anything you find cheap or things that are common may not really make you special or even add value to you. Many times, there are always bonanzas for knowledge so that people are able to get it either for free or at cheap price or with little sacrifice. Nevertheless, that does not make it common because there is always grace for everything. Grace is like a chance or opportunity given to people in order to possess or meet or pursue something.

58. It cannot die: Knowledge can never die because it is life given to people to live. Any attempt to kill or silence knowledge is like kicking against the goads. Knowledge is life because it proceeds from God. Knowledge can live for a long time beyond men's age. A particular knowledge can be obtained now and will live till the end of the world. This is the truth. A good example is Bible knowledge that

still exists and will be effective even till eternity because it is the Word of God. Other knowledge is that obtained through science and is still existing. The reason why knowledge is considered as dead sometimes is that it is not accepted or used by people, and sometimes the part of knowledge obtained may not be enough or useful to tackle hard thing, but that doesn't mean it's dead. You must understand that knowledge gives out every day, and also, knowledge is a source itself that gives out other ones. A genuine knowledge is life that kills death and ignorance. Any knowledge that dies is counterfeit.

59. It can expire depending on type and level of knowledge: Different levels of knowledge are needed to approach different problems as day passes. The part of knowledge obtained today maybe the one needed today or tomorrow. And if not used, it may not be useful another time as another level of knowledge will be needed to survive the next level of life. However, there are some parts or level of knowledge that we get now and will be needed in everyday life and in all areas of life. A different day requires different knowledge to survive it. Let me explain this to you in a better way. For example, the level one knowledge may only be effective to tackle the stage one of your life. Definitely, you will need another level of knowledge to survive another stage of your life as the one used in stage one may not be effective enough to win the battle in stage three of your life. But that does not mean the knowledge you got in stage one is dead, because it is a seed sown to you and is now contributing to your living. Take a

look at this again, the weapons used to fight in the eighteenth century will not be expected to be used in fighting in this twenty-first century because the level of knowledge used then has been upgraded to a higher level to produce a better weapon. Nevertheless, it is still the same knowledge that gave the solution in the eighteenth century is also giving the one now but in different levels. I believe you have understood that.

60. It can be rejected or neglected by one, that is, it is optional: Knowledge is very essential and also optional. It is something needed to survive, but it is not mandatory for you to take it. You can choose to have it or leave it. Knowledge will never force you to have it. As I am saying now, I can't force you to get the knowledge, but the best I can do is to encourage you. It is left for you to take it or leave it. God Himself doesn't force anyone. He shows you life. It will now depend on whether you want it or you prefer death (Deut. 11:26).

61. It can be made functionless if not used: It is very possible to have knowledge without using it. It is like having a key to a door without using it. In such case, ignorance is already in the bosom of the person and is ready to destroy him or her. Another good example is like someone having a cure to his or her sickness. The cure will be useless if he or she did not use it, and the sickness may finally kill the person. It is ignorance that makes knowledge to be useless or functionless in people's life.

62. It makes one to be perfect: When knowledge is properly applied, it will make the user a perfect person. Knowledge brings perfection. You can't expect an ignorant person to be perfect in good

things. Perfection is as a result of knowledge applied to produce excellence and exactness.

63. It can save a whole community, life, nation, and world: As I have told you when I was discussing the truths about ignorance that it can destroy a whole nation, likewise, knowledge can also save a whole community, life, nation, and world from destruction. When knowledge is effective and reigns in a place, it changes its nature, eradicates poverty, saves people from dying like fowl, and improves its economy. Communities, nations, and places that lack knowledge are always in danger.

64. It can be transferred: Knowledge can be transferred from one person to another and from one generation to another. Mostly, the knowledge in use nowadays was transferred from the past generation. A teacher is made to transfer knowledge he or she has known to his or her students. As you are reading this book, I'm transferring knowledge to you. Knowledge is shared in love and is also received in love. You can't get knowledge from people you hate neither can you give knowledge to people you hate. Any knowledge kept to one's self without sharing will be shared by another person. Knowledge is a spirit. As it comes to you, it also visits some people with the same information. Sharing the knowledge you have will be a privilege and honor to you that you're the first person to share that kind of thing. Haven't you noticed that other people or person also thinks the exact things you are thinking? That is, it is like you both have the same thoughts or ideas in mind. That is the reason you must try and be the first to share the knowledge so that others

won't take the honor that is supposed to belong to you. You must share the knowledge you have so that others can gain, and by doing that, you will receive the honor. I'm not saying you should tell people your secrets. What I'm saying is that a well-developed knowledge should be shared so that others will benefit. Examples of well-developed knowledge I'm saying are information, talents or gifts, skills, inventions, and other things needed by people to survive and that will improve the lives or world.

65. It can come as parable or plain words: Most of the time, knowledge comes in parables and is very hard to understand. Also, it comes as plain or simple words that are easy to understand. Whichever way it appears to you, you need understanding to be able to comprehend it and the wisdom to use it rightly.

66. It's useful and helpful in all areas of life: No knowledge is a waste. That is, all knowledge obtained is useful and has something to do in your life. We encounter problems in almost all areas of life, and the solution to all these problems encountered can only be provided by knowledge. You will definitely need knowledge to cope with any place, profession, and environment you find yourself in. The only time when knowledge will no longer be useful is when one is dead. But, as much as you are still breathing, you need knowledge in all your endeavors.

67. It determines how far you will go: The question of how far you will go in life, in your career, and in all your endeavors can only be answered by your level of knowledge. Knowledge is the fuel to the

engine of one's life. Once the fuel is cut off, the engine stops working. Likewise, if there is enough fuel to power the engine, the body is able to go as far as its capacity could carry. It does not matter where you start the journey, but your destination and success matter the most. However, where you start determines the level, quality, and amount of knowledge needed to reach your goals. A person coming from a very illiterate environment has much work to do with knowledge than a person coming from a well-developed place. If the person coming from a very illiterate environment can fuel his engine of his life with enough knowledge, he will arrive at a good destination and even go as far to rewrite the history of his environment, place, and family. Likewise, if a person from a well-developed environment powers his engine with a little knowledge, he can end up becoming a servant to the person who understands the usefulness of knowledge and has made it his friend.

68. Little knowledge may not be enough and can also change one's life to better: Like what I just illustrated in the previous number, where you are going in life determines the amount or level of knowledge needed. Although little knowledge can change some life to better, it may also not be enough to carry another to a place of destiny. If 5 liters of fuel is needed to travel a journey of 100 km, it may not be enough to travel the journey of 150 km. However, once you know where you are going, you will know and always refill your fuel (knowledge) whenever it is getting off. That is the reason why it is very dangerous to compare your

life with others. It is because you have different assignment to fulfill on earth and also you are coming from different background or family or places. You can relate with others to learn from them, but make sure you focus on your own destiny and journey of life. Don't be carried away with what others are doing so that you now neglect your own life and destiny. Check and work on yourself.

69.　It is hated by most: We will be lying if we should conclude that everybody loves knowledge. I tell you, many hate knowledge. In fact, the number of people who hate it is much more than the number of people who loves it. The devil has carried out his job so well that he has bombarded and blinded many people with ignorance so that they will always run away from knowledge rather than seeking it. You must understand that the devil hates you because you are created in God's image and you have been given authority to rule over him and other creatures (Gen. 1:28). He deceived our first father Adam, and mankind lost the authority to him. But thanks be to God that He did not leave us to be destroyed by Satan. God has outpoured His knowledge so that we can know Him (God) and recover all that the devil has stolen away from us through ignorance. The devil knew this and the only way to prevent man from knowing God so that they recover all and gain life is to make use of ignorance to blind man from recognizing knowledge, talk less of getting it. Devil himself is a liar and father of it (John 8:44). He made counterfeit knowledge and gave to people for free so that their eyes won't be opened to even think of the true and genuine knowledge from God. The best way to explain this is that people prefer to choose lie rather than truth and prefer to tell lies rather than the truth. Many hate truth because it will always scourge for correction.

70. It dwells inside man: Man is a home for knowledge. That is why God says His people perish because of lack of knowledge (Hosea 4:6). This means the knowledge that is supposed to be inside them is already missing. Man is made to be the citadel of knowledge. Animals are not supposed to take your place or tell you the right thing to do or teach you (Num. 22:23). Neither is any other creatures are supposed to take your place. Knowledge dwells inside man and has helped to invent technologies, do exploits, create ideas, and tame and control animals and other things. When you lack knowledge, you give animals and other creatures to take your place as knowledge carrier.

71. It requires hardworking and diligence: Working with knowledge requires hardworking and diligence. Diligence and hardworking are two of the many characteristics of people that are knowledgeable. Knowledgeable people understand the divine principle that those who do not work should not eat (Thess. 3:10) and that God will always bless the work of our hands (Deut. 28:12). In addition, from the beginning, men have been cursed to till the ground (that is to work) before he could eat (Gen. 3:17). Knowledge is not for lazy people.

72. The greatest knowledge that can be obtained is through the studying of the word of God: Other knowledge apart from the divine knowledge is

ignorance. Knowledge of God comes as principles or natural and spiritual. Both can be found only in His word which is the Bible. The Bible is the book written by the holy men of God through the inspiration of the Holy Spirit. Every true knowledge has its source from the Bible. If you need divine and genuine knowledge, you need to search through the Bible. Reading the Bible letters some time may not help (2 Cor. 3:6). But the true way to get the deep and golden one is to seek the Creator and source of knowledge Himself (God) before searching through. When you seek God first, He will put you through and show you the right one you need. He will interpret them to you and give you wisdom and power to make use of them. And sometimes He can speak to you. Yes, God speaks to man as man speaks to man. He can speak to your heart. He can speak to you in dreams and can also speak audibly to you that you will hear as if someone beside is talking to you (Exod. 20:19, Deut. 4:33, Deut. 5:26, Job 33:14). If you want God to be speaking to you, then you have to be His friend by moving close to Him, studying His word, always being ready to hear from Him, and obeying His commandments. Many a times God speaks to people's heart because they have not grown spiritually to hear Him audibly. You may have noticed or be noticing something telling you in your mind not to do something that is wrong and rather telling you to do the right thing, and another thing telling you to do it that there is nothing wrong in doing it. What is telling you not to do wrong things is God speaking to your heart, and it is the devil telling you to proceed that nothing will happen to you. The reason why God is speaking to you at that moment is that He has given you grace to repent despite all your unrighteousness. He loves you and wants you to move close to Him. Please accept Him and allow Him into your life if you have noticed this, because there is danger (hell) awaiting anyone who rejects God. Truly, hell and heaven are real. So far you dream and see or feel spirits prove that there is life after death and is either in heaven with God or in hell with the devil. If you are willing to accept God's calling, please don't hesitate to pray the prayer of repentance in the last chapter of this book. This book is written to tell you the truth by teaching you the principle and spiritual part of life. It is to help you both physically and spiritually. I am assuring you that as soon as you accept Him (Jesus), you will begin to see changes and you will surely testify.

73. It is always loved by those who are addicted to it: I have already told you that knowledge is hated by most people. The only few who love knowledge are those who have become addicted to it. These kinds of people totally depend on it. They don't have choice than to be with it at all time, and they have been used to it. Those that are used to ignorance can never love knowledge. People who are ignorant hate knowledge although may claim to love. Knowledge is truth, so anyone who loves truth will love knowledge and anyone who hates truth will hate knowledge.

74. It does not create or give chance for excuse: Excuses are things spoken to justify yourself even when you are wrong. There are reasons for any

occurrence, but no excuse is allowed. Ignorant people are found to give excuses. When you are guilty of doing something, as a knowledgeable person, you accept your fault, face the consequence, and do the correction where needed so that you won't repeat such mistake anymore. But ignorance will make one to give excuses so as to free or escape punishments and deprive justice.

75. It makes one to learn in every circumstance and challenges: People of knowledge always learn new things in every situation, circumstances, and condition they find themselves. They believe anything that happen either to them or people around them is a lesson for them to learn. And by so doing, they get knowledge that helps them to survive their own time and not to make the mistake that have been made by others. When such people fail, they don't count themselves as failure but believe that it is an opportunity for them to do better and do greater things. They learn from their own and other's mistakes and failures. They count challenges as an opportunity to learn.

76. It is not noisy but mostly silent or gentle: As I have sighted an example earlier, it is only an empty container that sounds when touched or hit. But a filled one will always remain calm when hit with a great force. Any person who is truly filled with knowledge is always gentle. That doesn't make him or her dull. The peace inside which is produced by knowledge in him will definitely reflect in his outward character. Knowledge is not noisy but gentle. It is ignorance that is noisy.

77. It is always sought by those who value it: Just like what is said previously that knowledge is

sought by those who love it, it is also sought by those who value it. That is, it is only people who really understand the mystery behind knowledge know it's important and who understand it's worth seeking it. Loving knowledge is different from knowing its value. To love means to adore and care, while to value means to know its worth, cost, price, significance, and importance. This should tell us that it is not all who love knowledge really value it, but those who value knowledge will always love it. It is possible to love knowledge in order to escape the danger of being ignorant but not truly understand its value to the point of claiming the benefits and good things inside knowledge. Let me explain that to you in a better way. It is like obeying law because you don't want to be guilty of the law; definitely, you will be forced to love the law. But you may not know the value behind obeying the law and even not claim the rightful benefit you deserve for your obedience. But all those who value knowledge will always love it more than those who just love it to escape the danger of being ignorant. But the truth is that those who love knowledge and not really value may fall because their love is not rigid enough to resist ignorance.

78. When knowledge is missing, life is missing: When knowledge is missing in one's life, what should be expected is death. When knowledge is absent, ignorance will definitely be present, and it does not have any good thing to offer than destruction. Knowledge is a powerful symbol of life and the absence of it is death. Death is not only physical death, but expiration of one's life and destiny, loss

of virtue or thing tangible in life, spiritual death, fall, downfall, ruin, overthrow, financial death, and so on. It is not only when someone gave up the ghost that he's dead. Some may have been dead for a long time while still living on earth. There are many that are working physically around us now but are dead inside or in other area. They are just like an empty vessel getting ready to be dumped. Any small thing kills them totally.

79. It is worth to be bought with great riches: Knowledge is so valuable that it is worth buying with billions or any other thing valuable to be sacrificed for it. It is of course expensive. Those who know the value of knowledge understand this and are always ready to sacrifice something tangible or valuable for knowledge. It is worth selling a whole mansion to get it. But the truth is that those who love riches cannot get knowledge and neither are they knowledgeable but ignorant. It is not possible to love riches and still expect knowledge to be your friend; you have to sacrifice one for another—riches for knowledge or knowledge for riches, because knowledge itself is very jealous. Once it comes in and dominates, it eradicates any other things contrary to and that are against it. However, it depends on the chance you give it. The reason why those who love riches can't get knowledge is that they won't be able to sacrifice valuable things for knowledge and be patient enough to get its reward.

80. It produces gain: No one has ever make use of knowledge and later regret except it is not applied with wisdom. That is, as I have already told you, you can't operate in knowledge without wisdom.

With the help of wisdom and understanding, you will know the kind and parts of knowledge needed and how to thoroughly apply them. Those who sacrifice valuable things like riches eventually end up in having true riches, honor, and every good thing you may talk of. True riches will come as a reward to the works of your hands with God's blessing that will give you peace.

81. Having knowledge is not a total solution, it must be applied: Knowledge is useless when it is not applied. When you get knowledge, you need wisdom and understanding to be able to apply it to the area concerned. When you have not applied the knowledge you got, you will still be at a state of ignorance because the knowledge is not controlling your life. Unapplied knowledge is like catching a fish by the tail, building castle in air, buying a brand-new car without testing, talk less of driving it or using it, cutting parts of a snake thinking it has been killed, dream about what you did not have, a king's son still controlled by servants and beating the air with seriousness. For you to be called a knowledgeable person, you need to apply the knowledge you've obtained. Or else, it will be like viewing what will save you from afar while something else is beside and killing you gradually. Knowledge is an authority that must be used.

82. It can live with one for years and remain useless when it is not in use or not considered or insulted: It is very possible to have gotten a particular area of knowledge for a long time ago without making use of it. At that moment, ignorance will have done much havoc and may have even killed the person. It is like being king's son

without exercising your authority while servants or strangers continue to maltreat you. It is like having a gun without shooting the enemies while still at the centre of the battle. Many people have access to knowledge, and in fact, we can say the knowledge is living with them, but they did not make use of it. For some, their father or mother or brother or sister or uncle or other relatives maybe a knowledgeable person, and that will have been an opportunity for them to tap into it, but they won't because they have been blinded by ignorance.

83. It does not require your position in order to be acquired: You don't need any position of authority before you will seek knowledge. The right time you need knowledge is now so that it will develop you and train you for the position you are looking up to. Your position does not make you qualify for it. As a matter of truth, it did not respect your position. If you need knowledge, you need to submit yourself totally to it (knowledge). In fact, you will need to sacrifice your honor for it by humbling yourself before you could get anything from knowledge.

84. Mostly, it does not require age in order to acquire: Your age sometimes determines your level of knowledge but not in all occasion. A small boy (a teenager) can be a tutor for the men who are over fifty years of age. In fact, Jesus begins to learn and ask question from the elders in temple when He was just twelve (Luke 2:46). Anyone of any age who seeks knowledge is qualified to have it. Only that a small boy may not be capable of withstanding the knowledge obtained without enough wisdom. But the rule behind knowledge is that all who seek it will find it. What most of the

elders called knowledge are experiences which may be accumulation of ignorance. I am not disputing the fact that the elders are knowledgeable, but what I am saying is that not all elders are knowledgeable. Some or most are ignorant and they will only have their experience based on ignorance. Age matters sometimes but is not really a barrier for getting knowledge.

85. Its presence is not really appreciated as when it is absent: Nothing good is appreciated when still present. We know value of good things at their absence. Many don't really appreciate knowledge, and like I have said earlier, many don't truly understand its value to man. When it is absent for a while, it is then they know its value. Just like a very good and generous person is not appreciated at his presence. But people feel his absence and understand his work and values.

86. In sight of a fool, it is valueless and useless: Knowledge is rubbish in the sight of a fool. A fool has already been doomed by ignorance. Fools mock knowledge. They don't value it at all and they see it as a hindrance to their lustful desire or fun. It is very easy to recognize or know a fool because they ever reject knowledge and truth. They love ignorance and lies with their whole heart.

87. It produces greater power: It is knowledge that produces the giant and powerful machines you can think of. Like caterpillars, they could destroy or uproot rocks, airplanes, electricity, and lot more. Development is as result of knowledge. Imagine how the world will be today without knowledge. It would have been void as it was in the beginning before God started the creation.

CHAPTER SEVEN

HOW TO GET KNOWLEDGE

In this chapter, I will be telling you the ways you can get knowledge if you need it. There are lot of ways in which one can get knowledge, but I will be mentioning as many as I can.

1. Be a learner: Learning is one of the ways of getting knowledge as I have said earlier. If you truly want knowledge, you must be ready to learn. Learners are leaders. When you don't learn as a servant, you can never in any way be a leader or master to someone else. When you learn, you gain both the knowledge and experiences needed to sustain you as a leader. A good learner is a fountain of knowledge. Learning in a simple terms or definition means acquiring knowledge. But for you to be a good learner, you need to be submissive to whosoever you want to get knowledge from. An arrogant person is not a good learner and can never get any knowledge except fake ones called ignorance. Through learning, you learn different form of knowledge that will make you a champion. If you are a student, prepare yourself and determine to learn from your education, teachers, parents, friends, environment, great men who have ever lived, and other things that will give you knowledge. If you are not a student, maybe you already have family or still single, you also

need to always learn from people, what you are doing, friends, tutors, elders, preachers or pastors, and other means you can get knowledge.

2.   Be a reader: When you learn from books you read, you will get knowledge. However, it depends on the type of book. If you are reading wrong books, you will only be accumulating ignorance that will kill you. Take time to avoid wrong books that can destroy and that teach unprofitable, useless, and ungodly things. The kind of book you read will definitely affect your life either positively or negatively. That is, if you read bad books, it will definitely drag you to the court of death because spirit of ignorance will be in charge. And if you read good ones that are profitable, it will always guide you to escape the danger of ignorance and the wickedness of the world. The kind of books you read will also determine your way of life, how far you will go in life, your life span, the kind of death that will kill you, your eternity, the kind of family you will have, your responsibility or attitude to your own people, your ignorance or knowledge, how foolish you are or wiser you are, whether you are or will be a champion, your relationship with God, your career, your priority, your future, and so on. It is worth making research on books before reading them because ones you get into some of those bad books, it won't be easy to come out. Some bad books even have good content in their cover page or in the beginning but pass their wicked and ignorant message at the middle to the end and by that time, to leave may not be easy because the mind would have been captured.

3. Be diligent: Diligence is highly recommended in the school of Knowledge. Diligence means persistent effort and hardworking. If you really want to get knowledge, you need to be steady until you get what is good. You need to be diligence despite problems and challenges. You must not be lazy nor should you lose hope. Persistency helps to get the best. You must not lose hope until you get the level of knowledge you need.

4. Fear God: The fear of the Lord is the beginning of wisdom (Ps. 111:10). A wise man will always seek after knowledge. Without wisdom, you won't even recognize knowledge, talk less of embracing it. The fear of the Lord will let you to abstain from evil and all ungodly things. And by so doing you will keep yourself from danger. Knowledge comes from God, and to have it, God Himself must be reverenced. You must also learn to fear God always if you want a genuine knowledge (Deut. 17:19). This is the truth you must know. Anyone who does not fear God is ignorant and not wise.

5. Always willing to take positive risk: When there is no risk, there cannot be a reward, and also when there is no retreat, there can be no surrender. Risk can be either positive or negative. A positive risk is like a challenge that when successfully met, it gives one a great victory and reward. While a negative risk is a danger that has no other result than death. For you to go through series of learning is a risk. It is a risk for you to even sleep in the night because many end up not waking up. It is a risk for you to go out in the morning because many went out without returning home. It is a risk for you to board a car or an airplane because many

boarded it and never got to their destination. It is a risk for you to marry because many have been killed by it. It is a risk for you to drink water and eat, because there is no assurance that it won't pass through your esophagus. It is a risk for you to stand up to pray, because many have stressed themselves when not fully awake and it affected them. Most of the things we do in life are risks. When you refuse to take risk, you should be ready to embrace dangers. The negative risk is what we should not try at all because the end of it is surely death. A good example is smoking and others things you may think of. (Also look forward to see our next publication on risks.) What I have being trying to say is that for you to get knowledge, you must take a positive risk to seek it and devout your time into it. You may not enjoy that moment of time devoted, but you will surely laugh in the end. Remember that when there is no risk, there can never be a reward.

6.   Buy it or purchase: There are aspects of knowledge you will need but needed to be bought. Don't worry about the price if truly you need it. Remember, I told you knowledge is worth buying with billions. No matter how much amount you used to get knowledge, you have not wasted your money. What you have just done is that you have invested the money for the future. It will surely yield a great multiple of what have been spent. But if you think knowledge is too costly to buy, try to do business with ignorance for few days and see what it (ignorance) will do with your life. No knowledge is costly. Any giver of knowledge has the right to sell what he or she has at any price.

But it is you who knows the importance of the knowledge and will take the risk to buy it at all cost not minding the price being sold.

7.   You can get it free, but with humility and hardworking or other sacrifice: Knowledge can also be obtained for free. When I say free, I mean without money or at low price. But getting it for free did not mean no sacrifice will be made to get it. The sacrifice may be your time, diligence, humility, persistency, etcetera. No knowledge goes for free. A sacrifice is needed to pay. Anything you get without any sacrifice can't yield you a lasting result. The sacrifice paid for it is just to show that you really need it and understand it values. But when you get it for free, without any sacrifice being made, you will easily lose it and ignorance may even kill you with it. Nevertheless, sacrificing other things for knowledge is better than using money to get it because you may not have money to buy it and may be ready to sacrifice all other things. A good example is a government school and a private school. A student who goes to government school can be a great man if he is ready to sacrifice his time for the knowledge. And likewise, a person who goes to private school may also become a great person in life and at the same time may not, depending on the sacrifice paid to show how serious he is.

8.   Long for it: Be persistent or have a strong desire for knowledge. Your strong desire for knowledge will show that you really need it. It is just like when we pray; you must have a strong desire and likewise be persistent before God will grant you your request. By this, you will be able to maintain what is given to you and also know its value. When you long for

knowledge, you will surely get it if you did not lose hope because sometimes, it may take time and lots of stress.

9. Create time to think and work things out: Man is made to be a good thinker. Knowledge can be obtained through thinking but depending on what you are thinking, lest, you get ignorance instead. When you think, you get the raw part of knowledge. It is then refined by practicing it, developing through more research and education, using it, working things out with it, and applying it. You will get new ideas when you think. You will always see the depth of a river when the water is settled and not when the water is being troubled. You will easily see what's on the bottom of the water when the water is settled. Likewise is man, when you create time to think, you will dig out creative ideas in you. But the ideas should be refined before it is used. This is the reason why many ideas are not valued or useful, because they are not attractive, that is they are still raw. If you are always busy to create time for thinking, you will always acquire ignorance. Imagination is formed through thinking. Vision or purpose can be obtained through thinking. Deep knowledge is obtained through thinking. It is what you think in your heart that you will have (Prov. 23:7).

10. Think positively: It does not end up in just thinking, but you must think positively. Think to provide solution to problems. Think to get new ideas that will benefit lives. An ignorant person will always think wrong things. It is exactly what you think that will happen. You need to think right to get right knowledge.

11. Love everybody. So far they are human: Most of knowledge is obtained from our fellow human. To love is a commandant from God (Mat. 22:39). Your neighbors or people who you hate may be the ones to help you out tomorrow. Don't love your dog and cat more than your fellow brethren. Cats and dogs can't help you when trouble comes; the only thing they will do is to bark and meow. What I am saying is that don't love animals or material things more than your fellow brethren. It is human being who will help you. Love is a seed that is sown for the day of harvest. Whatever things you get or face in the future is as a result of love you have sown. The knowledge you need can be obtained from human beings like you. Hating them will deprive you from getting the knowledge. You can't hate your tutor or teacher and expect to get knowledge from him or her. Love is an essential thing to survive in this life. There are situations that you face in this life that it is only the love you have shown to people in the past that will save you. (Acts 9:36-43).

12. Be a good listener: If you want to get knowledge, you must be swift to hear but slow to speak. This means, you need to pay a very good attention to knowledge instead of interrogating the tutor or trying to show that you know all. A knowledgeable person is a good listener. God gave you two open ears so that you can listen at all time. And He gave you one closed mouth so that you can open it to speak only when it is necessary. Always listen to people's knowledge, lectures, opinions, and ideas in order to acquire knowledge.

13. Get people's ideas or words: Most knowledge can be obtained from people's ideas and words. It may come in a written form or as lectures. Someone may have sat down to get a certain knowledge or it may be obtained through research and lots more, and the only way he or she can pass the knowledge is by speaking or writing or giving them out as ideas. When you get people's ideas, you will begin to learn better and even learn what you don't know.

14. Be submissive to teaching: For you to get knowledge, you must be an obedient student regardless of who you are. A good student is always submissive to teaching. A student is someone who is studying, and he or she can be called as a knowledgeable person. An arrogant or proud person can't get knowledge. For you to learn, you have to be under the authority of knowledge. It is an obedient student who receives knowledge. Be submissive to your teacher, your parents, tutors, and other people who are correcting you and teaching you. Submission is a good way to learn and to acquire knowledge.

15. Don't argue: Argument is as a result of ignorance, and as a matter of truth, knowledge should not be expected in place of argument. Don't argue with people, but rather listen to their words and opinion. Then later, you can go through and meditate on those words you've heard so as to be sure whether what have been spoken is true or false. You don't need to believe every word, but take the necessary ones you need and leave the rest. It will be very difficult for people who are found arguing to get knowledge. Argument

will only do nothing but shut up the mouth of knowledge and prevent it from speaking further. If you always argue with people, you need to check yourself because it is a symptom of ignorance.

16.   Don't feel to have known all: You must assume to have known nothing so as to get more and essential part of knowledge. Be humble enough to listen and learn from kids. Don't feel too big and to have known all that your kids or children will have no knowledge to offer you. I have said earlier that most of the elders are playing around in the school of ignorance while many young people and even children are doing great in the school of knowledge. That is why you could see many young people doing exploits. For you to learn new things, you will need to put aside all the ones you've known before so as to focus on what you need to know.

17.   Always be ready to accept it: Knowledge will always be ready to help you, but you must allow it if you want to get it. Knowledge makes itself known to people sometimes, and those who need it, accept it, while those who are ignorant, ignore it.

18.   Value the little you have and desire more: Learn to always appreciate the one you have. Don't be ungrateful to the little you have because it will hinder you from getting more. At the same time, always desire to get more. Don't be satisfied with the little you have so that you won't remain stagnant. Be thankful so that you can get more. If someone impacted you with knowledge, appreciate the person's efforts and gift, value what he gave you, and desire to get more from the person or others.

19.   Search for it: When knowledge is not available to you or is not at your reach, you need to search for

it. It is worth searching for because it is life. When you search for it with passion, you will surely find it, although it may take time and involve several sacrifice to be paid for it. It is not all knowledge that is available or easy to get. However, it depends on the types and level of the knowledge. Your location can determine an availability of knowledge. If knowledge is lacking in your present location, you need to go as far as you can to get it.

20. Learn from everything: Everything has lessons to pass across. That is, everything on this earth has one or more knowledge to pass across and which is always useful for us as human beings. Most of the time, in the Bible, God uses animal, plant, and other inanimate things to teach man lessons. He taught man not to worry about what to eat and wear by sighting an example of life of birds, lilies of the field, and grasses of the field (Matt. 6:25-34). There are other examples like that in the Bible. These actually show that there is lots of knowledge that can be obtained from everything God created on this earth just because God created all things for a purpose. You can derive knowledge when you study sand, stones, water, fire, and other things like that. Let me give you an example of knowledge obtained from studying water and fire. Water is friendly, useful, and can also destroy when made angry. No one can do without water. Water is essential for living. Fire is friendly, useful, and can also destroy. It is used for cooking. It is used for preservation and purification. It spreads and can go to extent where it could not be stopped. When you study them, there are lessons to derive from them.

21.   Study the word of God so that you can acquire divine knowledge: Knowledge is from God. The ultimate part or level of knowledge can only be obtained from His Word that is contained in the Bible. It is just like the knowledge I'm passing across to you; the truth is that I got this knowledge through the study of the word of God. Through studying and prayers, I move closer to God that He begins to reveal things to me. Part of the knowledge is what I'm sharing with you. There are upper parts of knowledge that may still contain some traces of ignorance. Just like a top of a soil, many things are found including dirt. But as you dig deeper, you will begin to see tangible things and valuable things according to their values in terms of their usefulness to man. It is only through the word of God that you can get the deep and most golden parts of knowledge. All other knowledge obtained is just common one that has been made available to everyone created on earth as guide and principle for their living. The secret and deeper part is only made available for the children of God so that they are the ones to pass it to the whole world. You must understand that secret things belong to God and those revealed belongs unto us (Deut. 29:29). That is the benefit of being sons and daughters of God because secret things that the world did not know is revealed to them by God so that the world will know those things through them. That is the reason why the Bible says that the world is waiting earnestly for the manifestation of the sons of God (Rom. 8:19). This means, the world is depending on the children of God for ultimate and uncommon parts

of knowledge so as to survive. Take time to study the Bible and not only read through it but study it. Before you read the Bible, pray that God should explain His word to you and open your eyes of understanding.

22.   Don't reject words without thinking about it: Don't try to overlook things or words without meditation. The knowledge you need may be present in those words you count as rubbish. Meditating on words will help you search through and to check if there are valuable or needful things in it. For example, if someone gives you some things that seem to be wastes, you may decide to throw them away because you think they are useless. But if you sit down and take time to search through those things before you dispose them, you may end up finding some useful things or valuable things in what you have called wastes. So also it is for words, ideas, books, and other things that may contain knowledge.

23.   Find a special time and a cool place to meditate: You must create time for yourself to meditate on what you gained or obtained so far. As I have told you, most of the knowledge obtained is sometimes in raw form. But the raw ones are needed to be refined and the ones that have been refined are needed to know where it should be used through wisdom. These processes must go through meditation. Meditation is the weapon of understanding. Meditation will help to get precious things out of the knowledge. It will help you to apply the knowledge properly. It will help you to fully understand the knowledge obtained, and it will help you to wisely make use of the knowledge.

24. Long to hear from God: God can teach and tell you what you don't know. God is the only One who knows all things including the ones we don't know. And every secret thing belongs to Him (Deut. 29:29). I have earlier on told you that God speaks to people, and you can even hear Him audibly depending on your closeness to Him. But the common ways He speaks to people is through the heart and dreams. When you seek God first and be in a good relationship with Him, He will tell and teach you mysteries the world did not even know. Good examples are Joseph and Daniel in the Bible (Gen. 37:5, Gen. 40:9, Dan. 2:19). God can tell you solutions to problems without passing through stress only if you are His son or daughter and know how to approach Him. You can also hear God through the ministration of the men of God.

25. Don't work with fools: There is a saying "Show me your friend and I will tell you who you are." When you work with fools, you will soon become one if you are not before. Foolishness is a product of ignorance. You can't be working with fools and expected to be wise. Fools are always found to reject knowledge and rather prefer to be ignorant. Fools are haters of knowledge. Fools are used as scapegoat for judgment and destruction. When you work with fools, they will make you to be like them. Evil communications corrupt good manners (1 Cor. 15:33).

26. Walk with people who are wise and wiser than you: See that you make wise people your friend. The wise will always seek for knowledge. When you walk with wise people, you will surely become

one of them. They will encourage you to seek knowledge when you are weak. Keeping company with the wise will give hope when there is none. When you walk with wise people, they will impact you with knowledge so that you too will become a knowledgeable person.

27. Be obedient: There are kinds of knowledge that can be obtained only through obedience. A disobedient child or student cannot get knowledge from his or her parent, tutor, and any other person. Disobedient is a product of ignorance, and it sets one into judgment of ignorance which is destruction. Walking with God requires obedience, less He destroys one (1 Kings 13:26). When you are obedient to authority, either of your parent or tutors, you make them happy that they will be ready to tell you more secrets and will impact you more with knowledge. Obedience will attract favor for you in the sight of people. Knowledge may be encamped in a command given to one or inside an authority in which you are under. When you are obedient to the commandments or the authority, the doors of knowledge will then be opened unto you through which you will need to walk through them. When you disobey someone who is supposed to give you the knowledge you need, you will be hijacked by ignorance.

28. Be a peacemaker: Violence is as a result of ignorance. Anyone who makes peace is knowledgeable. It is where peace dwells that knowledge can be found. When you make peace, you chase away ignorance so as to bring forth knowledge to dominate. At that time, you will begin to learn things under the

shadow of peace. For example, it will be impossible for you to learn where violence is occurring. Another example is when you settle a quarrel between two persons, then you will be able learn from both of them through their character and conversation probably with you. Those who make peace are called the sons of God (Matt. 5:9).

29. Always say the truth: If you want to get knowledge, you need to make it a habit and character to always say the truth. This is because the knowledge itself is true. When you keep saying the truth, you are creating chances and opening door for knowledge to come into your life. Truth will always justify you even before God. Liars are always condemned by knowledge. Knowledge always embraces the people who love truth.

30. Don't reject ideas: Opinions or suggestion of others may contain a hidden knowledge. That is why I told you earlier that you should not reject any words without going through them. Ideas are raw part of thinking. When they are properly refined, they become knowledge. That is why you should not reject ideas, opinions, suggestions, or plans, but rather take time to go through them so that you can get knowledge out of them.

31. Teach people: Most people don't know that the more knowledge you share with people, the more your knowledge increases. This life is based on the principle of giving which says givers shall never lack. When you give to people, you will open door for fresh things to replace the previous ones and you shall not lack the particular thing you gave out. But giving must be done with wisdom. When you teach others, it will help you to know

your worth, recognize your mistake, and study more to improve yourself. Apart from your own benefit, you will be able to satisfy others who thirst for knowledge because you become a fountain of knowledge to them. Let me give you a simple illustration to explain this better to you; can a fountain or spring of water get dry by giving out the water it has? No. Instead, it generates more as it releases some out. This is to say, the more you give, the more you get. The more you give out or teach people knowledge, the more you yourself will get. It is like when pointing one finger to a person, the remaining three will definitely point to you. This actually means giving out is not only good because you will be impacting lives but also good because it will give you an access to get more. How will the remaining three fingers point to you if you have not pointed one to someone or people?

32. Relate with people: Learn to relate with people because you will get knowledge from them. The more you are in relationship with people and especially knowledgeable people, the more knowledge you will get. Through your relationship with people, you will be able to know their thoughts and problems so as to give them the solution needed. Also when you relate with the right people, they will connect you to the source of knowledge, as it is impossible to reveal a secret, plans, and source to a stranger or someone you did not know. Relating with people has to be done with wisdom so that you won't fall into trap or trouble because of ignorance. Don't relate with a drunkard, smoker, or an angry person in such a way that they will destroy your life. You should

not relate with them so much so that they won't initiate you to the funs of ignorance. Although you can relate with them so as to change them, this has to be done with wisdom and you need to seek knowledge on how to go about it. The main thing is that you must not be equally yoked with them (2 Cor. 6:14). When you relate with people, you will learn from them either their character or the way of living. You don't need to do what they do as it may not be beneficial to you. But you will be able to express love so that knowledge will have an access to flow into your life either through them or from other source.

33. Study relevant things: There is some knowledge you won't get if you don't study hard or study things that are relevant. It is just like in the case of education. Through studying hard, you will dig in to the essential, expensive, and uncommon part of knowledge that will differentiate you from others. Hardworking people are always on top. But it is very possible to study so hard on useless things. And this actually brings pressure, wrong knowledge or ignorance, and wastage of time. You will need wisdom to know the type or part of knowledge you need before running after it.

34. Don't waste time on unnecessary issue: If you want to get knowledge, you must not permit nonsense and useless things. Knowledgeable people learn new thing every minute, hour, and day. Such people don't have time to waste. When you waste your time on unnecessary issues, it will fill your heart with ignorance so that it wastes your time. Remember I said in the beginning of this book that ignorance is like termite that descends on a

big tree. It gradually eats up the tree until the tree is totally destroyed. When someone wants to waste your time on useless things, try to excuse yourself because it is ignorance at work and will make you busy for him or her so as to create a very good platform for ignorance to feel comfortable in your life.

35. Pray to God, your creator: There are cases that need spiritual issue. This means the issue of knowledge and ignorance is a serious issue that man will need a supernatural or divine help from God. If you need wisdom or knowledge, then pray to God (James 1:5). God is the one who created all things and most of these things He created have been perverse by the devil. But He still has the original that He can still give out. Ignorance is a very strong force that God is needed to set one free. Our reference text says "God's people are perishing because of lack of knowledge" (Hosea 4:6). There are physical ways of getting knowledge, and there are ones you won't get from the world but can only be obtained from God. Remember I said knowledge is helpful and is a very essential part of life that is sustaining us for living. Solomon asked God for wisdom and understanding and God granted Him. The wisdom helped him to seek knowledge and also created a platform in which knowledge can dwell. The understanding explained all mysteries of knowledge to him that he became a fountain of knowledge during his own time. Even queen and kings came from far countries to hear from him. God knows the kind of knowledge you need and knows how to grant your request.

Chapter Eight

CONCLUSION

Let us go to the conclusion of the whole matter. The conclusion of all that we have being discussing is that knowledge and ignorance are the two common spirits affecting humanity. Ignorance destroys, and knowledge gives life. Ignorance is a spirit used by the devil to destroy mankind.

Knowledge comes from God. If you want knowledge to profit you, you will need to seek God Himself who created the knowledge. When you neglect God out of your living, you've neglected life and have just given devil a chance to do what he wishes with your life. Those who hate or neglect God are counted as wicked (Job 8:22, Ps. 9:17, Ps. 10:19, Ps. 50:16). And the Bible says God is angry with the wicked everyday (Ps. 7:11). It is a terrible thing to fall into the hands of the *Lord* (Heb. 10:31). If that should be the case, there is no need of seeking knowledge or trying to do anything better (Job 9:29) since God doesn't have any other judgment for the wicked than destruction (Ps. 9:5, Ps. 9:17, Ps. 37:20, Ps. 50:16). What this means is that if you are an enemy of God, despite the kinds of knowledge you've achieved in this world, you are still very close to destruction.

Beloved, I must tell you the truth. I have told you this book is written to help in both spiritual and physical aspect of life. God owns both (1 Cor. 15:45). You would have gained the principle of living which you can refer to as the physical aspect and may still need the spiritual part.

All what I have said in this book are principles to guide you from being ignorant, but if you are still an enemy of God, it may not help you to escape the torment of the devil. Or else God's mercy precedes; a knowledgeable person can end up dying like a fowl instead of an eagle. That is why you see people dying and being destroyed anyhow as if they are ant being trampled upon every day. And those we can refer to as a fountain of knowledge also die likewise and even more terrible because the greatest part of ignorance is inside them which is the lack of the knowledge of God.

What I am saying is that you may still end up in hell or fatal destruction of ignorance (despite all the knowledge obtained from this earth) if you are still an enemy of God. May be you have not given your life to Jesus or you are still toiling with sins. I have told you sin is a product of ignorance, and it destroys life little by little. It may look enjoyable now, but the end is always dangerous. I have stated this when I was telling you the truths about ignorance. If you truly want to enjoy the benefit of knowledge that entails peace, long life, and most especially sweet life in heaven (in the kingdom of God), you will need to accept Jesus as your personal Lord and savior. I must tell you the truth so that my conscience will be clear. The kingdom of God is the greatest inheritance someone can ever have.

The question that may arise in your heart is that what will be the benefit of accepting and knowing Jesus. Don't worry, I will tell you. That is why this book is a complete one. When you accept and confess Jesus as your Lord and savior, you will

1.   Begin to enjoy God's blessing.
2.   Become His friend
3.   Receive heavenly or divine instruction
4.   Become terror to ignorance and his master the devil
5.   Receive heavenly gift from God
6.   Be able to commune with God as with a Father and friend
7.   Ask anything you want from Him through the name of Jesus which will be granted.
8.   Be blessing to people
9.   Be a spiritual giant
10. Have spiritual power to overcome challenges or any spiritual and physical situation
11. Gain eternity
12. Be led by the Spirit of God
13. Able to make a decree and it will be established
14. Be a centre of excellence
15. Be a God's dwelling place that people will come to you because God is with you.

I have just mentioned few out of all the blessings you will enjoy if you accept Him into your life. And I am a very good witness. That is why I can write and teach you this knowledge.

If you want to accept Him into your life, say and confess this with your mouth, because God can see you and knows what is in your heart. So say it and confess with your whole heart.

Lord Jesus, I have come to you today. I now know that I am a sinner and I have cut short the glory of God over my life. I don't want to be your enemy any more. I have come like a prodigal son. Forgive me and accept me. Pardon me for all my unrighteousness. Cleanse me with your blood that you shed at the cross of Calvary. Have mercy on me and write my name in the book of life. Give me the grace to work with you, to live a righteous life and to always obey your voice. Thank you, Jesus, for accepting me today.

If you have just said that I congratulate you because God has heard you and you are now His child. You will begin to see changes in your life. Just make sure you listen to Him when he speaks to you as I told you earlier on that God speaks to man. He can speak to you in your heart. He can speak to you in dreams or vision and can speak to you audibly. Make it your daily activity to study the word of God which is the Bible. Pray to Him daily because He loves you and He wants you to commune with Him every time. Pray to Him to deliver you from the power of ignorance and give you the grace to seek and embrace knowledge. Try to always listen to the preaching of the men of God. Ask whatever you need from God in the name of Jesus and it will be granted onto you. Exercise your authority in Christ Jesus and desire to know Him more because He is real.

For questions and counseling,

Send an e-mail to:—truthandlifemotivation@hotmail.com
                    truthandlifemotivation@ymail.com

To get daily inspiring words, motivational words, and latest publication, like our facebook page truthandlife motivation

You can also send an e-mail to the author: etezekiel@ymail.com

You can also like his facebook page: E. T. Ezekiel